Some With HALOS Some With HORNS

A Family Journal

B.G. JERRY MICHIE

To order additional copies of this book, contact:
Xlibris
844-714-8691
www.Xlibris.com
Orders@Xlibris.com

ISBN: Softcover   978-1-6698-2581-4
        Hardcover   978-1-6698-2582-1
        EBook   978-1-6698-2580-7

Print information available on the last page

Rev. date: 07/14/2022

Foreword

By

Grace Renee Michie Bohl

My father had begun writing his book while wintering in our home in Arizona. However, he was never able to get it completed by the time he passed in February of 2008. Ever since his passing, I have fretted about getting his book completed. Well, with a lot of encouragement and assistance from my husband; I decided what better thing to do during the COVID pandemic of 2020 since I was unable to get out and do anything else. Also, I decided that the second half of the book should show how he evolved into the man that he became. I hope that those that knew my father enjoy reading this book and that it can also become a resource for our family generations down the road as to some of our family history. I would like to sincerely thank all of those that contributed stories about my father that I could insert in this book.

> *"No man's life can be encompassed in one telling. There is no way to give each year its allotted weight, to include each event, each person who helped to shape a lifetime. What can be done is to be faithful in spirit to the record and try to find one's way to the heart of the man…...*

> *Unknown*

Introduction

It's a helluva thing to look back and say the happiest time of your life was a time after your mother's death and during The Great Depression that had the country and my hometown in a death grip. However, nothing can change the memories of an idyllic time that stands out in my mind as pure joy and happiness. Nobody had anything, but you didn't need a whole lot either. My father saw to it that we had a roof over our heads, clothes on our backs, and food on the table.

The roof over our heads was a moderate middle-class home that housed my father and five brothers, any number of friends, a dog and, after my mother's death, a housekeeper to take care of the clothes and laundry and cook the food for the table. To say that it was a busy, much lived-in home would be putting it mildly.

Our good friends, J.C. Penney and Montgomery Ward supplied most of our clothes.

Being the fourth of five boys, I was a regular recipient of a time-honored practice known to the working class as "Hand-Me-Downs." I was 13 years old before I knew there were other kinds of pants besides corduroy and bibbed overalls. I was also 13 before I realized that someone other than Franklin Delano Roosevelt could be President of the United States.

When Dad hired a housekeeper to take care of us, little did anyone know how much we would all depend on her and her abilities. She was an old-fashioned lady with old-fashioned ways and religious beliefs. Along with all this came some good old-fashioned cooking that was just this side of heaven. The aromas that exuded from her kitchen (yes, her kitchen) were smells that only people of that time and era can remember and understand. Sometimes, in rare instances when the Gods are good, I can smell bread baking that comes close to what I'm talking about.

So, with the amenities of house, clothes, and food we had the home to live in, at a time that could only be described as the calm before the storm. It was a calm of wonderful carefree times where you enjoyed your family and friends, trusted your neighbors, made your own fun and pursued the happiness The Declaration of Independence called for. September 1938 starts the tale, December 7, 1941, and August 1946 interrupts it, and turning of the century ends it. I hope to take you back to those years and tell the story of my family and some.

Bibliography

David Francis Michie

Born 07-04-1886

Died 08-21-1946

Evangaline Lyons

Born 12-17-1884

Died 02-14-1930

Wedding 04-16-1906

Evangaline Ellen	Born 09-18-1907	Died 08-1-1980
David Francis, Jr.	Born 09-10-1909	Died 07-17-1910
Margret Mary (Marge)	Born 03-16-1911	Died 06-15-1989
Elizabeth Anne	Born 09-29-1912	Died 08-15-1915
Catherine Alyce	Born 03-28-1914	Died 08-11-1985
James Terrance	Born 11-20-1915	Died 05-05-1917
Agnes Rachael	Born 04-22-1917	Died 02 -?-1975
John Richard	Born 12-20-1918	Died 04-12-2000

Thomas Robert   Born 01-28-1920   Died 01-29-1965

Francis Aloysius   Born 12-05-1926   Died 12-09-1967

David Francis Michie   Grace Vivette Madden

Born 11-25-1900

Died 09-26-1938

Wedding 03-19-1931

Bernard Gerard (Jerry)   Born 01-26-1926   Died Feb. 19, 2008

David Francis Jr.   Born 09-03-1933

Chapter 1

SEPTEMBER 1938, RAWLINS, WYOMING

When someone dies and you are only six years old, the impact to your life is not immediate. Your memory is spotty, and you are not cognizant of the void created in your life and the effect it has on you from then on.

My mother was the center of my younger brother and my world. She taught us how to read and write. She taught us right from and wrong. And in between her illnesses, we played games and had fun in our daily routines. She was a good mother to her two sons. As a stepmother to my older brothers and sisters, it seems she left something to be desired.

My father had married and had ten children by his first wife (three did not reach maturity). His first wife, Evangaline, passed away after much suffering with rheumatoid arthritis leaving Dad a widower with six children. My oldest sister, Ellen, had married and was out of the home.

My mother, at this time, was studying at St. Mary's Convent in Leavenworth, Kansas, to become a nun. Before she took her final vows, she became ill and left the Convent to recuperate at her parent's home in Colorado Springs, Colorado. About this same time her father passed away and was buried there. Her mother (my grandmother) then married a man named Cleveland whose son, Pete, was married to my father's sister (Aunt Vee). My mother, also, had an aunt (Mary Callely) living in Rawlins, Wyoming.

Anyway, during her recuperation, my mother decided to visit her Aunt Mary Callely in Rawlins and while there, of course, met my father who was the brother of her stepbrother's wife.

David Frances Michie Sr.

Grace Vivette (Madden) Michie

Grace Vivette Madden married David Francis Michie in Lincoln, Nebraska, on March 19, 1931. To them were born Bernard Gerard Michie, January 26, 1932, and David Francis Michie, Jr., September 3, 1933.

Illness plagued my mother most of her married life, along with being a stepmother to two girls, Alice and Rachael, and three boys, John, Tom, and Francis. Marriage had left the family with a huge animosity toward their father and his new wife. Soon, Alice and Rachael left home and headed for California where Ellen and her family had moved. Was it because of my mother or was it time to leave the nest and head for the land of adventure and opportunity? Both sisters discussed this with me later in life and I suspect it was a little of both.

My father had a new wife with two new kids, and I can see how the older children would feel that their home and their family, as they knew it, was being invaded. Being a stepparent is hard at best and being a good one is almost impossible. There are always hidden resentments and the impression that parental love has been stolen by the intruder. It's been my observation on stepparents that there are fewer good ones than there are bad ones.

So, the older daughters departed their father's new family. They were old enough to go on their own, and they left to seek their own happiness. This was not the case for the older boys.

When I was born, John was 13, Tom was 12, and Francis was five years old. They were still suffering the loss of their mother, and the transition of a new woman in the house must have been a traumatic time for them emotionally; and I think it left unanswered hang-ups that followed them the rest of their lives. Needless to say, their relationship with my mother deteriorated to the point that both John and Tom left to join the Franklin Roosevelt's program the Civilian Conservation Corps (CCC).

Jerry and Mother   Jerry and Father

An emptiness in the home came with the departure of the older children.

We still did all the things kids do growing up until it was time to start school. But before we begin school, I must introduce an important addition to our family.

I remember, like it was yesterday, when Dad and Mom drove D.F. and me to Parco, Wyoming, and we got to pick our own little puppy from a litter of Irish Water Spaniels (some called them Irish Rat Tail Spaniels). I held him in my lap the seven miles back to Rawlins, and I've held him in my heart and memories all these years. We named him Duke, and he became a vital part of our lives. He roamed the neighborhood like a monarch overseeing his domain and accepted any gifts bestowed on him. He was always at the school when the bell rang to make sure D.F. and I got home all right. He was always ready to play any game we invented and became the best pillow while you laid on the front room floor listening to the radio. As a young boy, you have so many commitments in your life that you sometimes get sidetracked and take many important people and things for granted. You don't realize their importance until sadly these precious things are gone out of your life forever. This happened to me with my dog Duke. Apparently, Duke fell gravely ill, and my father and older brothers decided he should be put to sleep and out of his misery. I knew that Duke was getting older, but I didn't think he was that gravely ill. (I still don't.) My father decided to perform the deed and not tell me, thinking I suppose that it would be easier for me in the long run. My younger brother, D.F., told me now that he knew and watched while my father and brothers put Duke to sleep, probably with chloroform. One day soon after, of course, I came home and noticed my dog was not around. looked and called all through the house and basement and when I could not locate him in the yard, I became more than concerned because Duke was always there to greet me home and wag his tail. Dad, who was in his chair all the time I was calling my dog, asked me to sit down so he could talk to me. After he explained what had happened, I exploded. "Who do you think you are, God?" How could you do this to my dog? My dog, not yours. "Mine!" It was the worse confrontation I had ever had with my father. I never forgave him. My father was the foundation of my life, he gave me a basic honesty and fortitude that has saved me many times in moments of weakness and has sustained me through life and kept me on the straight and narrow. I loved and admired my father, as did many people and I will talk about him in this journal many more times; but with this instance of Duke, I never forgave him.

September 1938, I started first grade at the East Ward Grade School located at Colorado and Pine Streets. It was a four-room building that housed Grades 1 through 4. Each class had a room of its own; and, of course, there were hallways with drinking fountains and coat racks.

And a basement where the boys' and girls' lavatories were located along with storerooms and the boiler. The physical plant was not modern by any stretch of the imagination, but the mental plant was as good as it gets. In those four rooms in four years, I learned to write (by the Palmer Method, my kids must have learned by the chicken scratching method,) and I learned to read there. I learned basic math there, and geography, history, English, hygiene, music, manners, and how to get along with other people. That four-room building was the greatest learning institute that I ever attended. I learned enough there to carry me through the rest of my schooling and through life. Everyone continues to grow and learn but without the basics it's tough. Thank God for the old East Ward.

My mother died September 1938. She is buried in the Catholic Cemetery in Rawlins, Wyoming. My father had one of the first choices for lots in the cemetery, and I can remember him saying he picked his lots along the fence (next to the main highway) because he felt they would be seen by more people; therefore, the caretakers would always keep the area up. Over the years, I can honestly say the City of Rawlins does a good job keeping it a beautiful place.

Memorial Day services held at the "Rock" have had a special place in my memory.

After my mother's death, our home changed dramatically. My older brother, John, attended her funeral and stayed to finish high school. Tom (who was serving in the CCC's in Casper) was released and came home, also, to finish high school. They brought back to the home.

David Michie Sr and his five boys

A sense of vigor and vitality that perked our lives up immensely. They had left as boys and had come back as men. The Depression of the thirties did that to their generation and looking back, these Depression men were the backbone of our nation's effort that destroyed our enemies and won the Second World War. I'll get into that later.

John and Tom, as I said before, left home as boys and came back as men. They were both good big brothers to D.F. and me. The times before the war produced very little money to spend on things other than the necessities. So young people made their own fun and pursued pleasures that were simple uncomplicated and most of the time not harmful to other people and their property. Kick the Can needed, of course, a can. Anti Anti I Over, you needed a ball. Mumble Peg, you needed a pocketknife, and to knock on some neighbor's door and then run, you needed some swift feet, because some of the people would be waiting behind the door to chase you all over the neighborhood. Anyone who was around in the thirties seemed to know how to pitch Horseshoes with great accuracy. The best tosser in our family was John but then in those days every family had a best tosser in horseshoe pitching. Later in life this was very evident at every Elk, VFW, family or American Legion picnic or any other outdoor activity where they played horseshoes.

Generally, it was a Depression kid that found the old touch and waxed the rest of the new wave. Small town America September 1938 was still in process of recovery from the worst economic times this country had ever experienced. Rawlins, Wyoming, was no different than thousands of other towns throughout the country. There was very little money and if you had a job with a steady income, you were very fortunate. My Father, David F. Michie, was an Engineer on the Union Pacific Railroad (UPRR). He was the proudest man I have ever encountered in my life. He was proud of his work, of his family, of his country, and of his belief in God and His teachings. As Roman Catholics, we attended Mass every Sunday. In my lifetime, I have never seen a man or woman who lived up to the teachings of Jesus Christ and the Ten Commandments as well as my father did. There was never any doubt in anyone's mind who was the head of the house. At our house his name was Dave, and we called him Dad.

I will never forget once when some do-gooder ladies were out getting signatures on a petition to stop an afterhours roadhouse from acquiring a liquor license. Now my dad would never be caught dead in a place like that, but he would never stop anyone else from going there if it was their choice. Anyway, the three ladies approached the house feeling sure that Dave Michie would sign their sanctimonious petition. When Dad said, "No" one of the ladies asked, "But, Mr. Michie, why won't you sign?" and my dad looked her straight in the eyes and said, "I might want to go out there and have a drink sometime." Jefferson's pursuit of happiness perhaps?

Another true story of my dad involved a national contest on why you like a cold breakfast cereal. First prize was a brand-new car. Second prize was a brand-new aluminum bicycle. Dad wrote in that he was widower raising five boys, and he liked Friskie Wiskies because he could put them out for breakfast and then just leave them out for lunch. Well, lo and behold Dad won the second prize. We had the best bicycle in Rawlins, Wyoming. It was equipped with a light and a horn and the prettiest thing on two wheels. All of us kids were elated, but not Dad. His final words on the subject were "Damn it, if I had just left those Friskie Wiskies on for supper," I would have won the car. Well as I said before Father was a railroader, and we were railroad brats. The UPRR dominated our lives and all of us were geared to the 3rd and 18th of each month. The 3rd and 18th were significant because it was PAYDAY.

Dad's pocket money was carried in a deep pocket purse that had (as best I can describe it) ears. Two knobs that would twist apart and open the purse's mouth. Dad would then reach in and disperse the monthly allowance. Generally, it was one dollar to the elder brothers and fifty cents each to D. F. and me. I can remember D.F. and I being asked what we were going to do with our money. D.F. always said, "I'm going to save it;" and I always said, "I'm going to spend it." Somehow that philosophy has followed us somewhat throughout our lives.

Money is important in anyone's life and in the late thirty's money was a scarce commodity. Eleven cents (.11¢) would get you in the show (movie) and I remember the uproar when the theater owners raised the price of a ticket to 16 cents (.16¢). Nowadays movie tickets average around five dollars and with popcorn, candy and a soft drink you've spent most of a ten-dollar bill. The films aren't any better either. The shows in my hometown changed three times a week and the normal run was Sunday and Monday, Tuesday and Wednesday, and Thursday, Friday, and Saturday, with matinees on Saturday and Sunday. Once in a great while a movie would come along that would stand out as extra special. Such was the case in my youth with the film "Gone With The Wind." It captured my imagination and left a lasting impression on my young mind, and I have been a movie buff ever since. It also sparked an interest in History and the Civil War that has given me a lifetime of pleasure.

Back to money and the times. My father had many people come to visit him and always my older brothers would give them a special chair that sat across the room from my dad and his favorite chair. It was almost ceremonial and if any of us younger kids tried to sit there, John and Tom would shoo us out and make sure the visitor was seated in the place of honor. I never knew why until one evening Dad was out on the railroad and no one was in the house, and I happened into the front room. Here was John and Tom with the cushions out of the chair shaking it upside down. Man, it looked like Fort Knox! The change fell out on the floor, and they were splitting the loot. Apparently, the contour of the chair was such that anyone sitting in it contributed to John and Tom's piggy bank. Who knows how many nights out were paid for by those hospitable hustlers.

CHAPTER 2

JANUARY 1939

It's a sound you must hear for yourself to remember it. Any old-time railroader can verify it. Anyone who remembers steam engines must relish it. And if you grew up in Wyoming along any railroad it woke you up on many windy, cold winter mornings with its slow chugging and chugging as the big locomotive wheels would slip on the icy rails creating a swishing sound of spinning that can only be described a forlorn and lonely. After the first spin out, the engineer would try again and again to get the train in motion to pull out of the yards, crossover to the main line and on to its ultimate destination. Eventually, the train and its crew would be on their way and all of us would end up trying to get warm and then hit the bathroom for the quick wash and brush to get us ready for a breakfast of oatmeal and bread; OR oatmeal and milk; OR oatmeal and toast; OR, once in a while, lumpy cream of wheat. (I will not eat either one of them to this day.)

When there is one bathroom in a houseful of boys all getting ready for school, you have what could be called organized turmoil. Timing came into play and if you were last sometimes you washed and combed with cold water. The big brothers, of course, got first crack at the bathroom so I would settle for the bathtub. On my knees outside the bathtub, you could bend over and wash your head and neck and most of your upper body. Having taken a bath, the night before I could get in and out of the bathroom in pretty short order. Finding a spot at the mirror to comb your hair could be a problem but there were dresser mirrors back in the bedroom and your homemade haircut didn't need much combing anyway.

Rawlins High School (where John and Tom attended) was located about five blocks from our home and the junior high school occupied the semi basement level of the same building. My brother, Francis, was in junior high at that time. Anyway, off to school we would go, Monday through Friday. Everyone came home for dinner at noon and Mrs. Donahue would have a hot, nourishing meal ready for the onslaught. Dinner at noon and supper in the evening were two of the focal points of our lives. And, man, did we eat. Home cooked meals on an everyday basis is a thing of the past, but in those days, it was taken for granted. One rule applied though and that was take what you want, but if you take it you had to eat it. In other words, clean your plate because there were millions of people in the world starving to death, especially the Chinese.

I still clean my plate to this day. My father always said he would rather pay a grocery bill than a doctor bill. As I look back on the man, he paid a lot of both. The meals in our home were the times we had to share with our dad. Listening to his stories about growing up on a farm in Nebraska, about the railroad and life in general. These were golden moments and like all naive kids you don't appreciate it until the time and the person are gone.

Home cooked meals before the war usually meant home grown gardens, and we had one of the best. Maybe not the best (that distinction was held by two ladies of the neighborhood, Grandma Hood and Grandma Worth), but Dad grew raspberries, currants, crab apples, plums and rhubarb on one side of the backyard. On the other side he grew potatoes, corn, carrots, radishes, peas, beans and cabbages. (Yes, cabbages and there's a story about them later). He also grew horseradish, mint and other herbs scattered around the yard and believe it or not on the east fence he had a grape arbor and about every three years or so he would have grapes.

Grapes in Wyoming? Unheard of —but he had them, so help me, he did.

The coming of fall meant canning time. Mrs. Donahue canned most everything that was grown in the garden and a lot of other things bought in like peaches, tomatoes, beets, pickles, jellies and jams and sauerkraut. All these home canned goods were stored downstairs in the fruit cellar. The fruit cellar was a room in the basement that had shelves all around and before winter set in these shelves were jammed packed with all these goodies.

The food at our dinners and suppers while basically meat and potatoes always had homemade bread, all the milk you could drink and a lot of conversation. A family event that started with the Catholic blessing and then pass the gravy. One thing that stands out in my memory was that if anyone was in the house visiting or waiting for one of the kids, my father insisted that they had to sit down and eat. It was a time of sharing and sharing your food was a way of life, in our house at least.

Working on the railroad in the thirties was as good a job as you could get at the time. An engineer had the same romance as an airline pilot has today. I can remember the great steam engines pulling out of Rawlins with those unforgettable sounds bellowing out of their bellies.

We would park down by the cuts and wait till the big 4,000 pulled out of the east yards heading west to Green River, picking up speed till they reached us at the Cuts (named such because the railroad cut through a hill in West Rawlins leaving a cliff and thereafter called simply the Cuts.) When the engine passed by, the ground would shake, the steam would hiss and there like a God was my dad waving at us and giving us his whistle as he headed on out the cuts and onto his destination. We would wait until the whole train had passed and we could wave to the rear end crew in the caboose. Then they were gone, the ground was still, and we would go back to our everyday routines.

My father's railroading began in the town of Alliance, Nebraska, where he had hired out as a fireman on the Burlington Northern Railroad. He worked there for approximately two years until he realized that working on the Union Pacific was apparently a better job with more pay and better benefits. It was in Alliance that Dave and Evangaline lost their first child, a son, David Francis, Jr., during a flu epidemic in 1912. The records there show he was buried in the Catholic cemetery north of the town and separate from the Protestant cemetery east of the town. Dad never placed a monument over the little guy's grave, and I know it always bothered him that this was never done. (This was always on my mind, also, and one weekend in 1988, I drove to Alliance and with the great help of Charles Bilstien, the caretaker, we found the grave; and I had a tombstone placed on the grave. It was one of the most fulfilling things I have ever done in my life.

David Michie Sr's Big 4000

David Michie Sr. standing by train on the left

So, the Union Pacific hired Dad and his family moved to Rawlins, Wyoming, in the year of 1912. Early on they lost two more children, Elizabeth Anne in 1915 and James Terrence in 1917. Both were buried in the family plot in the Catholic section of the Ravenna, Nebraska, cemetery. If you have checked the births and deaths of the family registry you will see that every other one of the children died of an early age. That until my brother, John, was born and broke the chain. (John not only broke the chain, with him they threw away the mold, he is something special. I'll get to that later.)

Losing a child has got to tear your heart out. Losing three must test your very soul. Then to lose your wife would destroy most men. But most men were not made of the stuff that made up my father. Dad's first wife, Evangaline, passed away February 14, 1928, after a lengthy illness of arthritis. She was bedridden for the last five years of her life.

Death when it comes, can be so devastating because of the finality of it. You can't go back to the loved one who leaves you, to say the things that you feel you should have said before.

Always there is the initial shock that numbs your body and your senses. Then after time passes the real void of mourning sets in. Generally, the crowd has gone, and you are alone with your thoughts and memories. That's when you realize how much you miss the lost loved one. The two things that ease the agony of death are time and memories. Time passes, the pain eases, and your memories keep the love you have alive in your heart. The void never leaves, but you go on.

Death comes to everyone sooner or later. One can fear it, or one can choose to try and ignore it, but you certainly can't escape it. It's the ending process of life. So, my advice is live your life to the fullest, follow God's commandments, your fellow man and face death with the belief that you can meet your Maker knowing you did the best you could.

Dad wasn't a Fireman on the Union Pacific for very long. In less than a year, he was promoted to Engineer. This was because he had had previous experience on the Burlington. I've seen old seniority rosters that verify this fact. It, also, confuses me that he always belonged to the Fireman's Union and never the Engineers. In those days the train crews consisted of an Engineer, a Fireman, a Conductor and two Brakeman. One Brakeman rode the head end or the engine and the other one rode back in the Caboose with the Conductor. Anyway, they all had separate unions and it took some men of courage to participate in the labor movement. Dad jumped into the fray with both feet.

Our front room (living room to some) often seemed to be the meeting room of the Brotherhood of Local Firemen. Railroaders in the thirties and forties were a unique group of people. They would make their runs to Green River and back, get some sleep and then congregate somewhere close to the workplace and discuss their last trip from the start to the finish and all points in between names like Creston, Wamsutter, Tipton, Bitter Creek, Point of Rocks, and Thayer Junction rolled off their tongues with such frequency that if you were a railroad brat you knew exactly where and what they were talking about. Most of the railroaders of that time sought my father's advice on most anything that had to do with the railroad and the Company's rules and regulations. To most people on the railroad and in the town, he was Mr. Michie, and he took the time to try and help anyone who asked for it. One classic story about him had to do with a new and inquisitive fireman that continually bombarded Dad with questions like,"Mr. Michie, what should I do if this happens," and "What should I do if this valve doesn't work," all the way to Green River and back? Finally, as they neared Rawlins on the return trip, the brazed fireman asked, "Mr. Michie, what should I do if you had a heart attack and died?" My Dad looked him and answered, "Son, if I died of a heart attack here; I wouldn't give a damn what you did!"

The front room was, also, where the radio was in the house. When Dad's favorite show was on the air, kids had better be quiet or be gone. He had a great desire to hear the news. Every half hour he would find the news somewhere on the dial. I remember once Tom told Dad that the news didn't change that much during the evening and why not listen to something else for a change. Dad promptly informed him that it was his radio, and he would listen to whatever he wanted and if Tom wanted to listen to something else, he could go out and buy his own radio. The news continued to be listened to.

While we listened to all the radio greats of the time on a weekly basis, the voice I can remember most vividly was that of Franklin Delano Roosevelt. Radio must have been invented for him. Over the years, I have heard most all the orators of our time and F.D.R., in my mind, is head and shoulders above them. He had the public's ear, and he told them what they wanted to hear, and they loved it. His fireside chats were religiously heard in "our front room" along with millions of others. He gave people hope, and during the Depression that's about all a lot of people had. Roosevelt has had many critics as to his presidency and his programs, but I defy his detractors to say he couldn't communicate to the public over the airways. He had a voice that still captures my attention to this day whenever I hear it. In this journal of the thirties and the forties, Franklin Roosevelt will be mentioned again and again and again.

CHAPTER 3

DECEMBER 7, 1941

It was a rare American who woke up Sunday morning, December 7, 1941, and knew that Pearl Harbor existed let alone where it was located. However, when you went to bed that night it was a place and a date that you would remember and carry with you through the rest of your life. Sure, the world was in turmoil and Europe was at war, but what else was new, the Japanese were in Washington, D.C. talking peace and the hopes of most everyone in Rawlins, Wyoming, was that we could stay out of the fracas and carry on our idyllic life. Maybe we were all dreamers. Mostly, I think we were not informed, and no one cared about things that happened outside our little world.

The saying was never bet against Notre Dame, The New York Yankees, or Joe Louis. Joe Louis was the Boxing Heavyweight Champion, and he regularly annihilated his challengers with such ease that they were called, "Bums of the Month Club." Joe DiMaggio had hit safely in fifty-six games and a young cocky kid named Ted Williams batted 406 for the Boston Red Sox. Who cared about Poland or Czechoslovakia, and where was Indochina, anyway?

It was a cold brisk wintry day. Not a lot of snow, but you could feel the chill of winter setting in for its long seasonal stay. After mass and breakfast, I was playing out in the cold with Pat Noonan at his house, when Mrs. Noonan called Pat in, and I went home and entered the house through the back door. Everyone was in the front room sitting around the radio listening to the broadcaster announcing the sneak attack. No one spoke, and all ears heard the soon-to-be famous name Pearl Harbor. After the initial shock was over, I can remember my brother, Tom, telling Dad how we will whip those Japs in a matter of months. My Father looked at him knowing he would lose him soon and said, "Son, just take it easy, this war will take longer than you think; and there is plenty of time to join up." (You didn't enlist, you joined up.)

The tragedy of Pearl Harbor became even more personal when later it was learned that a local boy was lost on the U.S.S. Arizona. Richard Wallenstien's name is listed along with his 1,176 shipmates on the Memorial over the sunken ship. He was the first casualty of the war from our hometown. There would be many, many more, not only at home, but throughout the country.

Life as we knew it changed that day. No longer would we enjoy the innocent isolation. No longer could we expect the tranquil peace that prevailed throughout our great land. The guns of war were on us, and the future looked pretty dim.

The next day December 8th, 1941, the voice spoke to the nation again. Franklin D. Roosevelt addressed the Congress to ask that a State of War exist between the United States and the Empire of Japan. He called December 7, 1941, "A date which will live in infamy," and closed with the solemn affirmation that we would ultimately prevail. It certainly wasn't going to be easy and four days later Germany and Italy declared war on us, and the fat was in the fire.

F.D.R. called for a mobilization and a unity of the country that would have to be an effort unsurpassed by anything in our history. No one, let alone Roosevelt, could ever imagine the outpour of patriotism that surged forth from the American people. The Home Front as it was called began its transition almost overnight. Production switched from peacetime non-¬ essentials to wartime necessities. The two-hour attack on Hawaii did what Admiral Yamamoto feared. "They awoke a sleeping tiger and filled him with a great resolve." The rallying cry was "Remember Pearl Harbor," and we were ready for the fight.

The military, caught almost flat footed, took a little longer to get going because of the influx of men joining up for the duration of the war. They had to be trained, equipped and transported all over the country and the world. Still the young men joined up by the thousands.

The first to go from our family was Tom. He was scheduled to go in early 1942, but just before he was to leave (and celebrating too much with some of his buddies) the car he was riding in crashed, and Tom went through the windshield headfirst. His face was so severely cut that it took something over one hundred stitches to suture the cuts in his face. It left him badly scarred for the rest of his life. He was always self-conscious about is face from then on. My brother, John, believes the scars went deeper than his face. Along with the scars Tom had acquired another lifelong companion called alcohol. He didn't fight it, he enjoyed it. Somehow drinking soothed the demons that possessed him.

Tom left for the Army in the early 1940's. Life went on, but not as usual. Dad's job on the railroad was a vital link in the transportation of men and military equipment. Troop trains ran back and forth across the country and through our hometown on a constant basis.

Mostly boys on their way to become men or men on their one-way rendezvous with destiny can remember running errands for the men aboard the trains because they were not allowed to get down from the railroad cars. Usually, they wanted a bottle of whiskey from one of the many bars that bordered any railroad station. For these favors occasionally they would reward you with money or if you were lucky a sailor's hat. Any kid with a sailor's hat had a lot of status in my hometown.

My brother, John, was a fireman on the railroad at this time. He was happily married to his wife, Betty, and they had two young sons (Terry and Bill). Married men with two children were deferred from the draft so he didn't have to go, but as I said earlier patriotism was surging. I'm sure John weighed this over and over in his mind until he finally decided to enlist in the Navy in the early 1940's. He was the second one in our family to go off to war.

New words were coming into our language: Rationing, Scrap Drives, War Bonds, Uncle Sam Wants You, a slip of the lip can sink a ship and the worst word of the English language during those years "Hoarder." While things became harder to get, many people hadn't had a lot for the last ten years so a little shortage of things like sugar, gas, and shoes weren't so unbearable. However, when anyone was suspected of being a "Hoarder" their life could become so bad that in a popularity contest Adolph Hitler would lose to them.

Every school had a metal scrap pile. Of course, the high school was the biggest, and I suspect that it increased considerably during the night when the older kids would raid the grade schools' piles and transfer the scrap iron to their pile.

My Brother, Fran, was in High School at the time and, of course, chomping at the bit to get in the service and help win the war. By the time he was a senior in the fall of 1944, he was sure the war would be over before he could get into it, so on his 18th birthday, December 5th, he volunteered for the draft and was granted his wish to join the Marines. On the 20th of December 1944 he was the third one in our family to go off to war. His high school class graduated the next spring; and, by then, there were only two boys left in school to receive their diplomas.

The carefree happiness of our home was over. Those idyllic times of the late thirties and early forties would now become memories to cherish, but memories just the same. War had come into our lives, and things would never be the same again.

CHAPTER 4

WORLD WAR II, 1942-1945

Having passed the fourth grade at one of the three grade schools in Rawlins, everyone then attended the fifth and sixth grades at Central School. This meshed all the students together from all the areas of the town. No one knew what a school bus was and integration was accomplished without any government intervention. The rich kids from the west ward intermingled with the laboring kids from the east ward and the poor kids from across the tracks at the south ward. We all played together, studied together and learned together. That's not to say there wasn't an occasional fight at recess or after school, but once the fight was over you shook hands and generally became friends for life.

Fifth and sixth grades were, also, the years we heard the names such as, Guadalcanal, Midway, Coral Sea, Kasserine Pass, Sicily Salerno, and Ansio. We were taking the offense in the war, and America was producing the arms and materials needed to do the job. The home front was a beehive of activity and women were carrying most of the load. They rolled up their sleeves and went to work in the factories and the shipyards. Where they used to make cars, they now made tanks. Where they made lipstick containers, they now made machine gun bullets. Assembly lines poured out machines and material with a rapidity never seen by mankind before or since.

Everything was mobilized to support the war effort. The American women stepped up when it counted, and their efforts played a major part on the road to victory. "The sleeping tiger was awoken, and it was a female."

As the war progressed more place names were on everyone lips: Tarawa, Truk, Leyte, and Saipan in the Pacific and Normandy, St. Lo, Malmedy, and Bastogne in the European Campaign. Paris was liberated and halfway around the world the Yanks were storming Manila.

Christmas Eve in 1944 was bleak around our house. D.F. and I had already checked Dad's closet out and knew just about everything we were getting. We were home with Donnie (our housekeeper). Dad was out on the railroad; Tom was in the Philippines (after fighting in New Guinea) and John was on the high seas aboard the U.S.S. San Diego somewhere in the Pacific. Fran had left December 20th and was going through boot camp at Parris Island, South Carolina.

The Battle of the Bulge had been raging in Belgium. Hitler had made his last major assault and when it failed the war in Europe was in its final stages. This was not the case, however, in the Pacific. In the spring of 1945, the Marines landed on lwo Jima (February 19th); and U.S. Forces invaded Okinawa April 1st. John was there when the Kamikazes attacked the American fleet. Thankfully, his ship was not hit.

Franklin Delano Roosevelt died of a cerebral hemorrhage April 12, 1945, at Warm Springs, Georgia. The nation was stunned. We had attended a high school play and when it was over all the high school and junior high students went to their lockers to put on their coats and go home. The teachers were all crying and soon the news spread like a wildfire. The voice I had heard all my life was gone. I can't remember his inaugural address, but I do remember Fala and Barton, Martin and Fiske, but the one that stands out in my memory is his prayer on D-Day, the sixth of June. He looked so pale and tired in the newsreels when he came back from Yalta. We watched the newsreels closely in those days not so much for the war, but to see the West Point touchdown twins Blanhard and Davis perform feats of athletic splendor on the gridiron.

The newsreels carried the funeral procession in Washington, D.C. Grown men crying, women waving white handkerchiefs, the caisson carrying the President and the commentary by a little-known radio announcer, Arthur Godfrey. It was so sad. F.D.R. has had his detractors and maligners, but never from me. He led this country through its most trying times of the Depression,

and war. No man could have done more, and no man could have done it as well. We continually look for perfection in our elected leaders. Once elected, we continually look for their imperfections. In the world of countries, the United States is but a teenager and we act accordingly on a regular basis. Soon the reality of Roosevelt's death sank in, and the question on everyone's lips was, "Who the hell is Harry S. Truman?"

In May of 1945, I graduated from the eighth grade. My sister, Alyce, in California had two kids, and her husband was in North Africa and Italy flying missions. Of course, the war in Europe was over, but Joe (my brother-in-law) wasn't due home for some time. Dad thought it would be a good idea for me to go to California and help Alyce while she was alone with two kids. It was the start of a great adventure in my life. I was thirteen [13] years old, and I was going to Los Angeles, California, by myself.

Donnie put all the travel instructions in my autograph book (I still have it), and I left Rawlins Thursday, May 31st at 6:30 p.m. arriving at Union Station in Los Angeles Saturday, June 2, at 7:30 a.m. I took a taxi to the Pacific Electric Depot and boarded a bus and headed for Roscoe (now Sun Valley) where Alyce lived. The bus went through Glendale and Burbank before I got off at Gregg Avenue and had a short walk to her front door. About every other bus on that route detoured through the Lockheed Aircraft Plant. As it happened my first bus trip did this, and you can imagine a 13-year-old Wyoming boy traveling through a war plant that's under heavy camouflage with tight security. At the beginning of the war a budding aircraft industry exploded into the war effort, and here I was taking it all in. It's been over 50 years, but I can remember like it was yesterday.

By 1945 certain men of destiny had become famous for their leadership of the Armies and Navies of our country. Names that are part of history now, but back then they were our heroes: Marshall and King and Arnold in Washington, D.C.; MacArthur, Nimitz, and Halsey in the Pacific and Eisenhower, Bradley and Patton in Europe. All had played major roles toward the defeat of our enemies and all had become household names. One would make a lasting impression on me.

Jerry's Eighth grade graduation picture

CHAPTER 5

ALYCE

My earliest recollection of my sister, Alyce, was when she and my brother, John, returned home for my mother's funeral. She appeared again with her new husband, Joe Wendling, a couple of years later. Joe made a great impression on all of us. He had played football for the Milwaukee State Teachers College and gave us a leather game football as a present. Every kid in the town of Rawlins played touch with that overworked ball. The next time I saw Alyce was when I knocked on her door June 2, 1945. She immediately took me into her life, and I fell under her spell. They say blood is thicker than water, and they are right. It was the first involvement I had ever had with any of my sisters. Later in life, I became closer to my other three sisters, but Alyce was the first one to treat me like I didn't have a cold.

Catherine Alyce Michie was born March 28, 1914, in Rawlins, Wyoming. She was the fifth child of Dave and Evangaline Michie. She graduated from Rawlins High School with the Class of 1932. Her first marriage was to James Sommers and her first son, Fred, was born in 1936. Soon after, Alyce divorced James and supported herself and small son as a waitress in and around the Los Angeles area. Alyce never located too far from her older sister, Ellen; and I imagine, Freddie spent as much time at Ellen's as he did at home Times had to be tough and big sister looked out for little sister. Alyce met Joe Wendling while he was washing dishes at the restaurant she was working at the time. They were married in 1941. To this union was born Pidge Wendling in 1944 and Joseph Patrick Wendling in 1946. During the war Joe was first sent to North Africa by Lockheed Aircraft (who he was employed by) to service their aircraft and report back any modifications needed. When he returned to the USA, he immediately joined the Army Air Force and was sent back to North Africa for the duration of the war. Alyce maintained the home, took care of the kids, waited and worried.

One morning during my stay Alyce told Freddie and I to go down to the Burbank City Hall to see General Patton and General Doolittle. They were both Southern California boys and were on a War Bond Drive in the greater Los Angeles area. The drive would end up that evening at the Coliseum, and during the day they made appearances around the area, one of them being Burbank. Freddie and I maneuvered around trees and under ropes to where we could shake their hands as they made their way up to the speakers' platform. I can still see the motorcade coming up the street. Sirens blaring and the crowd going crazy. We got to shake their hand that day (I don't think anyone back home ever believed me) and both General Doolittle and General Patton gave a short address. Doolittle spoke about the great endeavor of the American people and how we would ultimately prevail in the war. General Patton rose and said, "You give me the Goddamn tanks and the Goddamn men, and I'll run those sons a bitch's clear to Tokyo and back." It brought the house down and the crowd to its feet, and it made a lasting impression on a boy from Wyoming.

Alyce was the first of my older sisters that I really got acquainted with after I was starting to grow up. I remember she was the only sister that came to my mother's funeral and a bond between us must have started then. She truthfully cared about us and showed it, time after time. Whenever any of her brothers showed up at her door, the welcome mat was always out.

Generally, we showed up with a buddy and they were, also, welcomed. Hospitality from your sister is one thing, but when it comes to your brother-in-law that's a different matter altogether.

Joe Wendling came from the East and had that bravado common to the region and the times. He did have a chip on his shoulder, but he could back up most of what he said. This was true while he was young and when he started to grow older, the bravado was still there, and as his dreams of fortunes waned, Joe kept up a front that was easily seen through. With all his gruff exterior, he had a heart of gold. I think the true test of friendship is knowing the friends' faults and still liking him. Along with Alyce, Joe always made me feel welcome in his home, and I loved him very much.

Joe and Alyce had a host of friends in and around Burbank. Especially when they were running a bar. And, for the most of their life together, that's what they did. When I was old enough, tending bar for them was an experience I thoroughly enjoyed. Meeting the parade of characters that came and went through their place was an education that Harvard and Oxford could never hope to teach or understand. I could never put my finger on the common denominator of all these characters, but my best guess was Joe was the 'Pied Piper of Lonely Souls.' They came to California looking for whatever and found the substance of nothing. They would never go back to wherever, and by staying they would never quite find the dream they were seeking. With all the trips I've had to California, I have always returned to Wyoming with its sense of values, it's four seasons, and its people boldly facing the reality of life.

JERRY'S SISTERS

Left to right: Marge, Alyce and Rachel

Left to right: Ellen, stepmother, Alyce, Rachel and her husband, George (1947)

JERRY'S SISTERS

Ellen and Alyce

Marge and husband, Clarence Crum

CHAPTER 6

MORE ADVENTURES

Riding a passenger train to California back in 1945 is an experience at any age. Doing it by yourself at 13 is an adventure most kids only dream about. The war in Europe was over, and America was mobilizing on the West Coast to eventually win the war in the Pacific. Railroads were the vital movers of the men and machinery needed to do that job.

If you were a railroader's kid, you most likely traveled by rail on a pass. And on a pass, you had to ride the second-class passenger trains—no streamliners for the workers or their families. In 1945 these trains were jam-packed with servicemen, wives, and kids of servicemen and the general public. When you found a seat, you staked a claim and settled in. I was lucky that whenever I showed the Conductor my dad's Railroad Pass, he recognized the name and would make sure I was looked after. Dad's reputation as a labor leader followed me to Los Angeles and back, "Are you Dave Michie's boy?" was a question I was to answer most of my adult life.

In the summer of 1945, Wyoming was as war weary as any state in the Union. The young men were all gone, people were tired of rationing and, more importantly, tired of the ever-increasing numbers of war casualties. America hadn't suffered losses like these since the Civil War. The war in Europe was over, but the big job was yet to come: the invasion of Japan. How many more Americans lives would it take for that great endeavor? America knew it would be costly and was geared for it. They didn't like it, but they knew it had to be done.

After returning home from California in late July, I ended up scooping winter wheat on a farm outside Encampment and Riverside, Wyoming, in Southeast Carbon County. As I said, there were no young men to bring the crops in, so it fell on old men, women, and kids to do it. Sunup to sundown scooping wheat, I was scooping wheat in my sleep. I was probably scooping wheat when the Enola Gay took off from Tenian Island. Two bombs were dropped, and the War was over. I've never scooped wheat since. I never will!

The War was over. Wahoo! What do we do now? Kid, you go back to school. John, Tom and Fran will be coming home. Soon things will get back to normal and when the last son gets home, we will celebrate the victory and ask God's blessing for a future of peace and happiness.

John was the first son home. He had served honorably aboard the U.S.S. Cruiser San Diego (the first ship in Tokyo Bay) and was back home with his wife, Betty, and their two sons, Terry and Billy. He would go back to work on the railroad and return to the normal routine of his life, loving and caring for his family, working for his church and helping anyone who needed it.

Tom was the next son home. He had seen action at New Guinea and the Philippines and had served honorably in both areas. When I hugged him, you could smell the pungent order of alcohol on his breath. He was back home with no wife or family. He would go back to work on the railroad and return to the normal routine of his life—drinking, fighting and staring in the bar mirror looking at his scarred face. He never went to church, and my dad was very worried and concerned about him. More on Tom in his Chapter.

Both John and Tom came home in 1945. Before Fran got home in August 1946 a couple of things happened that were important in our lives. I was in the eighth grade and D.F. was in the seventh grade and the big event of the school year was the Southwest District Basketball Tournament. In those days it was held every year in Green River, Wyoming, and it was the big event of the school year. When I was in the seventh grade, I was too young to go, so now in the eighth grade I could go; but guess what, D.F. who was now in the seventh grade could go with me because I would be there to take care of him. "I want to go, too," was always the words D.F. uttered whenever I would to do anything. So, D.F. and I took Dad's pass and rode the train to Green River. Lo and behold who was there to meet us but Dad. He showed us the depot, the club, the restaurants he ate in, and the room he rented where we were to sleep. All this time I was anxious to get to the gym because Rawlins was beating Green River, and I was missing it. Dad finally walked us up the hill to the high school, and we got there just in time to miss the game. remember being very irritated at my father then. Now, I'd give up any game of any kind if I could relive those precious moments.

In July 1945 Dad had planned a trip back to Lincoln, Nebraska, and wanted D.F. and me to come with him. I had a job flagging trucks that summer and making good money. I didn't want to go to Nebraska and told him so. When the time to leave was getting closer, I received a letter from Aunt Maggie Curran in Lincoln telling me that I was hurting my father's feelings, and I should reconsider coming to Nebraska. I couldn't for the life of me understand why it was so important for me to make the trip, but if everyone wanted me to go then no big deal, I'd go.

On the train just before we got to Lincoln, it was made perfectly clear why Dad wanted us to accompany him. He was heading for his third wedding. To say that D.F. and I were surprised would be putting it mildly.

Soon we were all caught up in the wedding festivities, and we were never close to our father again. Dad was sixty years old and his new wife, Margaret, must have been fifty-eight. She was, also, from Ravenna, Nebraska, and they had been childhood friends (maybe more than that).

After the wedding and the honeymoon, we all settled in at home and things got back to normal. No one knew our lives were about to take a devastating blow.

Fran came home August 1946, and my dad was elated. Everyone in the family finally had the onus of war off our shoulders and out of our minds. The day was joyous and then the phone rang. Dad was called for his run on the railroad. Never missing many runs, he told us that he'd make this trip to Green River and back; and then, we would have a celebration to end all celebrations. Dad saw Fran for about an hour and then went to work. Fran went downtown and proceeded to get drunk with his buddies.

I was sleeping with Fran the next morning when our stepmother tried to wake us up with news and said she was leaving to go somewhere. D.F was the one who finally got me awake and told me Dad had been in a train wreck during the night and had been taken to the miner's hospital in Rock Springs. We tried to get Fran up again, but to no avail (alcohol was dictating his life even then, but we didn't discover that fact until later).

We learned later that dad's engine had jumped the tracks on a curve at a section called Thayer Junction, just east of the Town of Superior's turn off. The steam had scalded him very badly and he was in critical condition. My brother, John, had left with my stepmother Margaret earlier in the morning to go and be with him. Tom had been on a train behind Dad, so he hopped off his train in Rock Springs and was the first to get to the hospital. D.F. and I were driven to the hospital by Bill West who was brother John's father-in-law. I can remember the first sight I saw was Tom sitting in a chair across from the foot of the bed. He was sobbing in his handkerchief. You could sense he realized the seriousness of a death watch. As I approached the bed, Dad winked at me and said, "He hasn't got me, yet!" Those were the last words he ever spoke to me.

Dad died on August 21, 1946, apparently the severe burns caused his kidneys to collapse, and he was gone. His funeral was held at St. Joseph's Catholic Church where we had all been baptized, had our first communion and were all confirmed there. The services [service was] were jammed, Father Gerard Shilling (who I was named after) celebrated the mass and his eulogy was the best I have ever heard. It was the first time I had ever seen grown men cry. Our family rock was gone and those that tried to take his place were little pebbles, especially our stepmother, Margaret. I didn't like her the first time I saw her and for the unhappiness she brought to our lives after my father's death; I can forgive her, but I still don't like her.

The wreckage of David Michie Sr's train (1946)

CHAPTER 7

TOM

When Tom was born the doctor didn't get there in time, so my father had to deliver him. Dad always said that he should have cut the umbilical cord sooner because he gave the kid just too much blood. Didn't Jesus change his blood into wine? Well, whether he had too much blood or not, Tom's life was a case study in alcohol and the inner demons that followed him to the end.

Growing up in Rawlins, Wyoming, in the 1920's and 1930's and at the tail end of a large family had to be rural and austere with plenty of time for kids to be active and mischievous.

It seems as kids, whatever John did, Tom would follow along and be a part of any adventure John would dream up. The stories are numerous, and I will relate some of them later. So, when John decided to leave home so did Tom. He joined the CCC and was posted at Saratoga, WY, and then later at Casper, WY. Friends of mine have told me many people would go to CCC boxing matches just to see Tom fight. In the ring, Tom didn't box, he fought like a wild animal. Fist fighting was a way of life in those days, and you were a small celebrity if you could get it on with your fists. Manhood demanded it, and Rawlins, Wyoming, had a well-known reputation for its bars and its street fights.

When John and Tom came back to the home to finish high school, they came back as men rather than boys; and they had some living to do. Dad had a 1936 Buick automobile which took abuse not meant for ordinary cars. Basically, the only time Dad drove the car was to church on Sunday morning. Many times, the old car would run out of gas going up the hill between home and the church. Needless to say, Dad was never too happy. On the Saturday night before, John and Tom must have coasted or pushed the car in the garage, knowing the gas gauge was on empty.

Tom played good football in high school. He was known as a tough runner and hard-headed tackler. One of his teammates described scrimmaging against Tom as it always hurt. Because he dropped out of school for two years, by the time he was a senior he was too old to compete in high school athletics. This left a lot of time in his life for partying and girls, which also meant drinking. A habit that would follow him the rest of his life.

After the start of World War Two, Tom was scheduled to enter the service in the spring of 1942. Just before he was to leave, he was severely injured in a car wreck. He was in the passenger side of the front seat and was thrown through the windshield severely cutting his face so badly that it took over one hundred stitches to close the lacerations. My brother John believes Tom's scars were a significant down factor to his self-esteem that followed him the rest of his life.

Tom recovered from his injuries and entered the Army in 1942. He served honorably in New Guinea and the Philippine Islands in the Pacific. Sometimes his letters would say he was a Sergeant then back to Private then up to a Corporal and back to Private and so on. Most of the excuses to Dad had to do with alcohol.

After the war, Tom continued to work on the railroad as a fireman and spent his leisure hours supporting the bar owners on Front and Fourth Streets. Rawlins, Wyoming, had public bars in 1946 and all of them were concentrated in one area of town. This area also had six houses of ill repute, four restaurants, and the Union Pacific Depot. All this activity was encompassed on two blocks of Front Street and one block of Fourth Street perpendicular to Front Street.

He met one of the 'Ladies of the Night' and continued his descent with his demons. Looking back, he was doomed from the time he took his first drink of alcohol. When his "lady" finally left, more than alcohol was involved. Drugs were not common at that time, but they were around and I believe that Tom was deeply dependent on them. Everyone in our family was busy with their own lives and couldn't see the warning signs of Tom's problems.

A local bar owner began to brag in front of Tom about his exploits with Tom's wife and how much a better man he was. In January of 1950, Tom took a gun (that he bought the day before) walked into the Wyoming Bar and shot Morris Larson six times killing him almost instantly. He then sat down at the bar and waited for the police to arrive.

My younger brother D.F. and Mr. Larson's son Dick were in the same classroom at school when they came to tell them what had happened. Dickie Larson, D.F. and I were all on the Rawlins High School Basketball Team. Larsons lived only one block away from us. It was devastating to both families.

Tom's trial in June was a highly visible and publicized event for our small town. After a sanity trial, the jury found Tom sane, and he then plead guilty to second degree murder and was sentenced to 25 years in the Penitentiary. After five years and good behavior Tom was paroled with a warning by the then Governor Millard Simpson that he'd better not screw up or he would answer to him personally. Governor Simpson was the Father [father] of U.S. Senator Alan Simpson and Peter Simpson, who I later served with in the Wyoming State Legislature.

Tom met and married again to a girl from Chicago named Pat. They had two girls. After he got off his parole, they moved to Chicago and on the night of January 29, 1965, his car skidded on some ice and hit a stationary post. Tom was killed when his head smashed against the windshield. He is buried in the Resurrection Cemetery, Chicago, Illinois. God rest his soul.

Tom and his wife, Pat (1963)

CHAPTER 8

HIGH SCHOOL

Trying to cope with the loss of your father and living with a stepmother who knew nothing of raising kids was to say the least an unhappy experience. The high school years should be a carefree time in life that readies you for the outside cruel world. D.F. and I lived inside a cruel world most of our teenage years, with a stepmother who outwardly seemed to be a sainted person stepping in to raise two orphaned boys. The truth of the matter was that as long as she took care of us as our guardian, she would receive a monthly check from the railroad and live in the house until we were through college. This woman was the greediest person I have ever encountered. She beat the other children out of their share of the property by right of possession after the other members of the family agreed to allow her to live in the house if she maintained a home for the minor children (D.F. and me.) She acquired full ownership of the house after ten years by right of possession.

We had no money for ourselves, no allowance, not very many clothes, and the meals she prepared were something out of a poor farm. She couldn't cook, but she could sure count the money. As I look back there were two things that got us through those trying years—athletics and our brother Fran.

Football was my life. We played it anytime the weather permitted. We played on the Courthouse lawn, the Penitentiary lawn, in the street, and sometimes even in the front room of our house.

Rawlins High School had a resurgence in athletics during the 1940's. It was due to some great coaches and some great talent that the little town produced. Whenever your role models are athletes, just about every kid in the town would try to emulate them. Of course, I was caught up in that kind of passion and it was the reason you went to school because school was where these great events took place. You also tried to keep your grades up so you would be eligible to play these great games. As a sophomore in high school, I could look forward to a lot of scrimmages and not much action in the regular games. I didn't care, I was part of the team special things were going to happen.

Then our stepmother dropped her bomb. D.F. and I were going to be shipped out to Regis High School in Denver. The dreaded Catholic school run by the Jesuits. My world was crushed. My hopes and dreams were with Rawlins High School! How could she do this to me. We had already started practice; I was going to be second string. My God, how could she do this? I'm not going!

I ran away from home. She had the police bring me home. But I still wasn't going. She had the Priest Father Shillinger come and practically order me there. I still wasn't going. She had my brothers, who I loved, talk to me. Nope, I'm not going. Finally, she went to the Coach just before the first game and he sat me down and told me that I should go because I wasn't going to play that much for another year. Anyway, I was devastated. This was the year I would join the R. Club, the ultimate for any Rawlins athlete.

Defeated I gave in and consented to go to Regis in Denver. She had won the battle, but she hadn't won the war. Not just yet. I didn't like her from the first time I saw her, now I hated her.

Regis was a Catholic college and high school for men. It was run by the Jesuit Order of the church. It was located at 50th and Lowell in 1947 (the high school has since been moved) and looking at it for the first time one would think it a normal academic learning center. Regis had a reputation of a great school. Little did I know that its rules and regulations would be tough on a kid that was used to running his own life. Also, I soon learned the difference between the day students and the boarders—those students who lived on campus and lived with the priests and those who were about to be priests.

The day students were under the control of the Jesuits from the first class in the morning until the last class in the afternoon, Monday through Friday. The Boarders were under the Jesuits control from the first day of school, till you left at the end of the school year (at least you got to go home at Christmas).

I could never understand the Catholic school system and I still can't. I think most of their goals were first to recruit men for the priesthood and if they were not inclined to be priests, then to be blindly faithful believers and obey the church laws and live a good Christian life. When I asked questions about this I was soon looked upon as a troublemaker and shouldn't be asking questions about things that were over my head.

Blind faith is great for some, but not for me. I had two eyes and could see what was going on around me. So, I kept these thoughts and doubts to myself just to pass the year, go back to Rawlins and pick my life up where I left it.

Now I look back and wonder how these men ever thought they could be priests. I will never know. Living with them you found them mean, vindictive, and self-important. My respect for priests fell to a new low. I never lost my faith in God or the church for that matter. Some of the human beings that promote their own agenda and take advantage of the youth are being found out and hopefully the church will survive and carry on the Christian belief as it should be.

After the school year, D.F. and I were home and putting our lives back together. My stepmother received a letter from the Superintendent at Regis. He welcomed back D.F. for the next year. After his signature there was a P.S. that said under no circumstances will your son, Jerry, be allowed to return to this school.

I was overjoyed. I could return to Rawlins High School, keep my eligibility to play football and never see Regis again. I thought I could finally find some happiness in my final two years. Little did I know that happiness did not come pre-planned.

Jerry in leather jacket

Senior pictures of basketball and football

CHAPTER 9

FRANCIS

Everyone called him Fran. He had the brightest red hair I have ever seen in my life. He was about halfway between John and Tom and D.F. and me. Most of his short life he was trying to live up to John and Tom, especially Tom. And the other part of his life was trying to live it down.

Fran was born while his mother was bedridden with crippling rheumatoid arthritis. Rumors were his birth hastened her death, and Fran carried that guilt with him to his own grave. These demons were compounded with the ones of alcoholism. Whenever he drank, his personality changed from a happy-go-lucky, wonderful guy to a mean-spirited, mixed up, individual. Mixed-up to the point of embarrassment to the rest of the family.

But in his youth, everyone liked Fran. He was good to everyone around him and especially good to anyone younger than him. I think he knew how tough it was to compete in the world with people older and stronger than you are. Whenever there was a bully pushing littler kids around, Fran would be there to take care of him.

When I grew up in Rawlins, Wyoming, you had to learn to defend yourself or else. Fist fighting was a way of life, and kids were taught how to fight from the first grade on. The strong of body were the Kings of the playground, and those that made it an even playing field were everyone's hero. Fran always made sure things were even-steven in a fight.

He was small in stature, and he had some big shoes to fill in our family if he was to become as tough as John and Tom. They were double tough. Neither one was a big man, middleweights mostly, but tough as nails. This was the image Fran tried to live up to and he could never quite measure up to the other two and it became an obsession that he never could conquer. He thought he had to fight, drink, play athletics, and show his courage because of his name. Had he just been his own self, with his own personality and his own goals; he could have conquered the world.

None of my older brothers ever got to finish their athletic careers in high school. John and Tom because of their age, having dropped out of school for two years. Fran because of missing practice his senior year while working on a ranch. Subsequently he enlisted in the service on his 18th birthday, December 5, 1944. Of course, to show his courage he volunteered for the Marines. The war ended with Fran serving in Hawaii getting ready to invade the mainland of Japan. John and Tom had come home after seeing a lot of action in combat. Fran came home and saw his father for about an hour before Dad went off to his death. This scarred him deeply and I'm sure preyed on his mind until his own death.

Nothing, of course, was ever the same after the war. Dad's death left a void that was never filled, and Rawlins became the party town of the western world. Fourth and Front Street had eleven or twelve bars going practically all the time. The second stories over half of the bars had houses of ill repute with ladies of the night, waiting for their customers, and in the back of almost all the bars there were gambling tables waiting for the same customers.

John had a wife and kids and was not caught up in the phony glitter of downtown. The same can't be said of Tom and Fran. Tom with his scarred face and Fran with is scarred psyche were like moths drawn to the flame. Alcohol was their companion, and despair and destruction were their destiny.

Before Fran was discharged in 1946, he knew there would never be another war so why not join the reserves. A lot of World War II vets had done the same thing. They got the biggest surprise of their lives the summer of 1950 when the North Koreans invaded South Korea. "I've been called up!" was the cry heard throughout the country. Fran went back to the Marines in 1950 and after a short combat training course at Camp Pendleton was on his way to Korea.

I was in Navy boot camp in San Diego, California, just before Fran shipped out for Korea and we got to see each other one night on the town. I remember he was still the happy go lucky guy everyone loved. I was still in San Diego when he came back, and it was obvious he was not the same guy. I believe he saw too much war. He would never say what had happened, but from then on Fran had a dark side, and brooded privately with his demons. Alcohol continued to be his companion.

His life deteriorated more with a failed romance, after years of wandering, his life ended in Chicago, Illinois. He had fallen asleep with a cigarette, probably drunk, and before anyone could get to him, he was burned over 90% of his body. He passed away three weeks later. Fran is buried in the Michie plot in the Rawlins Cemetery. He's in my mind and memories.

Francis Aloysius Michie

CHAPTER 10

LIFE IN RAWLINS

High School should be one of the happiest times of your life. It should be, but when you start as a freshman with your father dying and you end your senior year with your brother killing a man, it drains a lot of the joy you should have at that time of your life. Compound those two bookends of time with the fact that in between those bookends you are living with a penny-pinching stepmother, you have all the elements of delinquency. Had it not been for athletics, I probably would have ended up in the penitentiary. Growing up in Rawlins you never wanted to be called a sissy, and the best way to show your manhood was to participate in sports, football especially

I'm a good example of what can happen with a little talent, persistence and practice, practice, and more practice. My dream was to run for a touchdown at Outlaw Bowl. To me that was the most ultimate achievement. Nothing could ever top that. So, I dedicated myself to football in the seventh grade. That, also, was about the time my dedication to classroom work and grades started to wane.

My stepmother interrupted my Rawlins athletic career my sophomore year by shipping D.F. and I off to Regis in Denver. However, I was back in Rawlins my junior and senior year and by the fall of 1949, I was the starting left halfback on the Rawlins Outlaw Football Team. Man, I had reached the pinnacle; and my dreams were achieved. During that season I played pretty good football and by the time Outlaw Day (our homecoming) came around, the coach gave me extra duties. Now let me explain here that whenever we played, my brother John and his wife Betty were always there. The only problem with John was I could never do anything right. After a game I always got "you should have done this" or "you should have done that."

Outlaw Day October 1949, Rawlins was playing a tough Sheridan Team and they had a kid who had returned kick offs back for touchdowns three or four times. So, our Coach Joe Schwartz told me to lay back on kickoffs so I could catch him and save a touchdown against us. That game was one of the best I had ever played. I ran for a touchdown, intercepted passes, made a lot of tackles and as it turned out the kid from Sheridan did break out and I caught him to save a score. Now I knew John had to say that I played a pretty good game and as we came off the field there he was. He said and I quote, "Well you played a pretty good game, but dammit you're lagging on kick offs, you've got to get down there and smash 'em before they get going and keep smashing them." I just turned and walked away. How can you argue with a big brother that has all the answers?

Jerry's High School Graduation picture (1950)

CHAPTER 11

JOHN

When John was born, they literally broke the mold our family made at least. You see after the oldest child was born (Ellen) every other sibling died in early childhood until John came along and lived to adulthood. Thereby, breaking the mold. He never let us forget it either.

My earliest memory of John was when I was four or five and he, Tom and Fran let me go with them to ice skate at the local rink. (Rink may just be the best way to describe it.) Basically, the city had banked a vacant half block and flooded it with water. The day we were there the weather had turned warmer and one end of the "Rink" had thawed a little. Of course, this was the end I skated for and promptly broke the ice and fell in. I was only four or five, it was still winter, and it was cold, and I went under. The next thing I remember my brother John was in the water picking me up and out of the freezing water. Tom was waiting on the bank to run me home. Apparently, Fran helped John out and they then ran for the heat of home. Big brothers are something special. Younger brothers get the benefit of their ground-breaking experience, and they also have them as critics for the rest of their lives. John as the oldest relished his role as oldest brother to the hilt. His advice was always listened to but seldom adhered to. He seemed to be a little tougher on his brothers, than on his own children. While we sometimes used passive resistance with some of his doctrines the fact of the matter was, he was he was always there of any of us.

He was there for Tom in all his troubles. He stood by him during his trial and incarceration. He stood by him when it was an unpopular thing to do. During that time, he kept the family together.

He was there for Fran during all his bouts with alcohol and mental depression. I can remember listening not saying a word when John talked to Fran like a loving brother about where he was going to end up unless he quit drinking. John of course knew that an alcoholic must want to help themselves before anyone else can help.

John went on to follow in his father's footsteps and worked as a railroad engineer. He also followed Dad as a union leader and worked tirelessly for the men and their working conditions. One story I can recall was a disgruntled railroader came into Rawlins in the middle of the night and received reprimand from the officials and their rules. The man not thinking about anyone but himself and knowing John was probably asleep called him anyway. John answered the phone listened to the man and told him he'd get to him in the next day or so.

John waited till the next night and set his alarm for the middle of the night, and then called the man back. Of course, the man had been sound asleep and wasn't told anything that couldn't have waited till the next day, but John made his point and the man apologized.

John is not easy to write about because I looked at him as a hero. In my life he took over the family on our dad's death. He did the best he could for all of us while he had his own wife and family to provide and care for. He did put too much trust in our stepmother who was paid by the Union Pacific Railroad to take care of D.F. and me. That being because we were minors.

In adulthood John came to about my shoulders in height. But he will forever be my Big Brother and one of my hero's. John died of a stroke on April 12, 2000. I miss him every day.

John Richard Michie

CHAPTER 12

D.F.

David Francis Michie, Jr., was the baby of the family and must have suffered the loss of his mother and father as much or more than the rest of the family. He had just turned five when his mother died and was only 12 when he lost his father.

As a youngster he was sickly and needed the security of the home and the love of our housekeeper Donnie. He was also the stubbornest.

Mrs. Donahue was a Seventh-day Adventist and regularly took D.F. to that church's services. Our Dad was a hard-shelled Catholic and demanded we attend the Catholic Church [church]. It was no problem for me because I was an altar boy and attended catechism to the point that Dad thought I might be a priest. So, all was well with me, but it wasn't quite the same with D.F.

Donnie's influence on D.F. was beginning to lean toward the Adventist belief to the point that one Saturday morning he told Dad he wasn't going to catechism. WOW!!! This was heresy. D.F. was told to go so he went to the top of the hill counted to a hundred and went back to the house and Dad. He gave D.F. one of the worst spankings he had ever had. D.F. never did go to catechism that day.

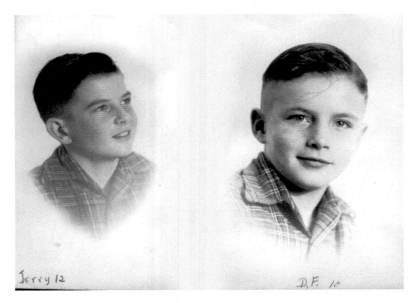

CHAPTER 13

THE NAVY IN PICTURES

Jerry on U.S.S. Newport

Navy enlistment and discharge.

Jerry's first ship U.S.S. Newport

Jerry first one in back row

Jerry lost his left eye in the "Battle of San Diego"

U.S.S. Sutherland

CHAPTER 14

FAMILY IN PICTURES

In 1958 Jerry met a dark-haired, blue-eyed beauty named Ida Lee Hopkins. The two were married in 1959. To them were born Grace Renee Michie, July 18, 1960, Bernard Gerard Michie, Jr., July 30, 1963, and Geneva Marie Michie, February 9, 1965. Their marriage only lasted until 1966 and he was awarded full custody of all three children.

Jerry in Sinclair, Wy with Renee, Jerry Jr. and Geneva

Grace Renee Michie

Jerry Jr and. Geneva

Geneva, Renee and Jerry Jr. as adults

Back row: Jerry and Renee

Front row: Geneva and Jerry Jr.

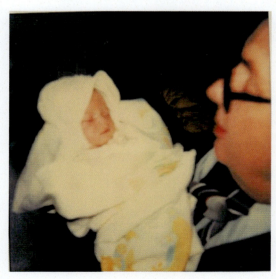

Jerry became a grandfather for the first time in 1982 (Jeremy). It would develop into a lifelong bond

Life in the U.S. Editor
Readers Digest
Pleasantville, New York 10570

    Recently my daughter asked if I could pick-up my two grand children (Jeremy and Heather) and give them a ride home from their day care center. I, as a doting grand father eagerly agreed and after work proceeded on my mission.

    After securing them in their seats, I thought about the quickest way to proceed to their home and decided to take a short cut through a parking lot, make a left turn at the street, miss most of the evening traffic and be headed straight for their home. Six year old Jeremy immeadiatly informed me that I was going the wrong way and not to cross the parking lot. I of course knew better and proceeded on to the street. Lo and behold it was a one-way street going the opposite direction for my left turn intentions. So then, in order to achieve my goal and direction, I had to make a right turn at the street, a right turn at the next corner another right at the next corner and still another right turn at the third corner. After the fourth right turn Jeremy looked up at me and said, "Gee Grandpa it looks like to me we're going around in SQUARES." And you know he was right, we were.

B.G."Jerry" Michie
409 W. 24th Street
Cheyenne, Wy 82001
1-307-638-2274 H
1-307-632-5409 O

Mailed October 3 , 1988

Jerry with granddaughter Heather and grandson Jeremy

Jerry with grandsons, Dillon and Jeremy

Christmas 1997

Christmas 1999

CHAPTER 15

PUBLIC SERVICE AND COMMUNITY ACTIVITIES

Jerry in the Wyoming State Legislature

Jerry's mentor Reno Hakala

Get out to Vote committee (1964)

United States Senate
WASHINGTON, D.C.

May 15, 1968

JOSEPH D. TYDINGS
MARYLAND

Mr. Jerry Mitchie
107 - N. 8th Street
Sinclair, Wyoming

Dear Jerry,

Just a few lines to tell you
how much I appreciated your hospitality
and the kindnesses extended to me last
Friday at the Wyoming State Democratic
Convention.

It was a most delightful sojourn
for me. I particularly enjoyed the
breakfast, meeting Jerry, Jr., and the
ride to the airport with you both.

Keep in touch with me and if you're
ever in Washington, stop by.

Best regards.

Sincerely,

Joseph D. Tydings

Copy to:
Hon. Robert F. Kennedy

Wyoming Democratic Convention 1968

United States Senate

COMMITTEE ON APPROPRIATIONS

WASHINGTON, D.C. 20510

May 20, 1968

Mr. Jerry Michie
107 North 8th
Sinclair, Wyoming 82334

Dear Jerry

Now that the excitement has somewhat subsided over the Vice President's visit to Rawlins May 10, I wanted to drop you a personal note to convey my thanks for the role you played in making the trip to Wyoming an outstanding success in every way.

The Vice President remarked again and again about the friendliness and warmth of the people of Rawlins. I know he'll never forget it, nor will I.

Thanks again.

Regards

GALE McGEE
United States Senator

dl

Democrats elect Michie as county chairman

Thursday, November 13, 1975—THE DAILY TIMES, Rawlins, Wyo.—2

Carbon County Treasurer B. G. "Jerry" Michie was elected Sunday as the chairman of the Carbon County Democratic Central Committee.

He replaces John Terrill, who did not seek reelection.

Michie has been active in the committee for a number of years, serving as vice-chairman and finance chairman, in addition to other posts.

Also elected to two-year posts Sunday were Delcy Moulder of Rawlins, vice-chairwoman; Mary Mann of Rawlins, secretary; and Edna Francis of Rawlins, treasurer.

Bill McIntosh, a rancher who lives north of Rawlins, was elected state committeeman, while Carolyn Gettman of Rawlins was chosen state committeewoman.

Michie, McIntosh and Mrs. Gettman will be traveling to Casper early next month as Carbon County delegates to the meeting of the Democratic Central Committee of Wyoming.

They will join other county representatives in electing state officers.

The Carbon County Democratic Central Committee holds no regular meetings, but according to Michie, "as we come closer to the elections of 1976, we will meet much more often."

The committee's goals, according to the new chairman, are to reelect U.S. Senator Gale McGee and U.S. Representative Teno Roncalio next year.

"Whether you agree with the seniority system or not, its still a

way of life in Washington, D.C. And both men, of course, hold a great deal of senority."

Other goals include the reelection of democrats to three courthouse positions to be vacant next year. Michie and County Commissioners Emil Lemich and John Orton, and Assessor

Darrel Stubbs will be up for election in 1976.

About his new position, Michie said "I'm looking forward to the chance to try to fill the shoes of some of my predecessors. I hope this can be accomplished. I also want to thank John Terrill for efforts put forth in the past."

Democrats...

Carbon County Treasurer B.G. "Jerry" Michie (standing) is shown here with John Terrill, who he replaces as chairman of the Carbon County Democratic Central Committee. Terrill chose not to seek re-election, and Michie was elected Sunday to the two-year position.

Oct. 26 - 77

County Treasurer resigns

Carbon County Treasurer Jerry Michie submits his letter of resignation to Commission Chairman John Glode during a special meeting yesterday afternoon. Michie's resignation, for which he cited salary and family obligations as reasons, will become effective Nov. 1.

CC Treasurer Michie resigns; cites finances

Carbon County Treasurer Jerry Michie submitted his resignation to the county commissioners yesterday afternoon blaming cost of living and family obligations.

MICHIE'S RESIGNATION will be effective Tuesday, Nov. 1, and, according to the commissioners, no one has been named to replace him. Michie has served as county treasurer since 1969, and has a year left in his second term of office.

"Family obligations are my first priority and with the cost of living escalating I have to make a move that I can hopefully make a living at," Michie explained.

Michie said he will be purchasing a private business, the Stockman's Palace Bar on Front Street. "Public service is rewarding, but not financially," he added.

"When a person is responsible for $16 million a year, he should be adequately compensated," Michie said, concerning his $12,500 annual salary.

"I've enjoyed working for the county, and I've had the opportunity to work for two regimes. I've met some pretty wonderful people," he stated.

MICHIE SAID HE attempted to keep up with county growth during his eight years in office. He noted that the county was issuing 6,000 car passenger license plates in 1969, and are now issuing more than 16,000.

Commission Chairman John Glode asked, "What are we going to do for a treasurer around here?" The commissioners have one week to replace Michie.

Commissioner Mutt McMahon added, "Whoever replaces him will have to learn his job — and fast!"

County Assessor Darrell Stubbs said, "Personally I'm going to miss him a hell of a lot. He has been a lot of help to me."

Michie explained that he would be available to advise whomever the commissioners appoint to replace him.

Jerry serving in Wyoming Legislature

Jerry Michie elected president of NCCAE

CHEYENNE — B.G. "Jerry" Michie has been elected president of the National Council of County Association Executives at the group's recent annual meeting in Jackson.

Michie, who is executive director of the Wyoming County Commissioners Association, assumed his duties at the Jackson meeting and will serve for one year.

The NCCAE consists of county executives from 48 states and serves to provide a vehicle to improve county government and a forum for discussion of county government issues.

The Wyoming County Commissioners Association is part of the Wyoming Association of County Officials and both are affiliated with the National Association of County Officials.

Michie, a Rawlins native, has more than 30 years of public service, including two terms representing Carbon County in the Wyoming House of Representatives (1979-1981).

He previous served eight years as Carbon County treasurer and six years as deputy assessor of Carbon County. He was been executive director of WCCA since 1981.

Michie, 61, is a Navy veteran of the Korean Conflict and was educated at Montana State University, Denver University and the University of Wyoming. He has three children, Renee' Larson, Jerry Michie, Jr. and Geneva Karajanis.

B.G. "JERRY" MICHIE

Jerry Michie elected to NCCAC presidency

Jerry Michie, executive director of the Wyoming County Commissioner's Association (WCCA), was elected at the annual executive director's meeting in Minneapolis to serve a one-year term as president of the National Council of County Association Executive (NCCAC).

The NCCAC is a national association made up of county officials from 48 states and was begun for the express purpose of supporting and improving county government throughout the United States. The association suggests and lobbies for county-supportive legislation and, through an annual national convention, exchanges information and procedures that assist county governments to progress more efficiently.

The WCCA is a part of the Wyoming Association of County Officials (WACO) and both organizations are involved with the NCCAC.

Michie, whose 30 years of county government experience began as Carbon County assessor, has also served two terms with the state legislature. A resident of Cheyenne for 10 years, Michie is a Korean War veteran.

Bill signing with Governor Sullivan

Dedication of Independence Rock

Independence Rock

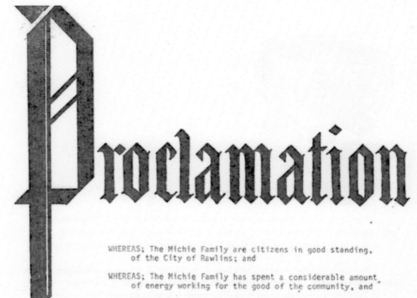

Proclamation

WHEREAS; The Michie Family are citizens in good standing,
of the City of Rawlins; and

WHEREAS; The Michie Family has spent a considerable amount
of energy working for the good of the community, and

WHEREAS; The Michie Family has contributed a great amount
of effort to the athletic activities in the City of
Rawlins by being deeply involved in youth baseball;

NOW, THEREFORE, I, Glen A. Woodbury, Mayor of Rawlins,
Wyoming, do hereby proclaim the

Northwest field, at VFW Ball Park, shall
be, and is hereby named The Michie Field,

and I do hereby urge all citizens to show their
appreciation and share in the tribute being
paid to one of our outstanding citizens.

IN WITNESS WHEREOF, I have hereunto set my hand this
8th day of June, 1983.

Glen A. Woodbury, Mayor

Dated: June 8, 1983

FORTY YEARS OF SERVICE

For Jerry "B.G" Michie, putting together the details of an "R" Club reunion program is more than a science or an art. It is a passion. It is a single-minded commitment to bringing together those who love, support and participate in sports.

For the past four decades, Jerry has made the "R" Club event so distinguished it has become a classic. Trying to recollect each detail from the three reunions (1970/1980/1990) that stretched over thirty years is next to impossible, but Jerry is a master at remembering names, addresses and reunion events. Most of us settle for tucking away a few outstanding highlights in our memory banks~ memories of our guest speakers, the great Jackie Robinson, the football stories of George Blanda, and Bob Mathias as the teenage Olympic decathlon champion. Yes, we can recall the milk-can dinner, dancing at the Elks Club, picnics, visiting home town sites and meeting friends at the Jeffrey Center, but Jerry is the one who can see the "big picture" and pull it all together. This year we will generate new pictures, new friends, relive yesteryear and share memories as old as the 70 plus years of the "R" Club.

Because of Jerry Michie, a special event is taking place in Rawlins. It takes shape in the retelling of lives lived and sports stories of firsthand knowledge that are passed from friend to friend. Considering his commitment to the preservation of the "R" Club, we owe our most sincere appreciation and thanks to Jerry for this millennium reunion and his years of service to sports.

From a lifelong friend,
Gary A. Eyre

THE 52ND PRESIDENTIAL INAUGURAL

AN AMERICAN REUNION

1993 COMMEMORATIVE INVITATION

On January 20, 1993, our nation celebrates its Fifty-Second Presidential Inauguration. Americans join together to witness their President take a simple thirty-five word oath of office and witness the triumph of representative democracy through the peaceful transfer of political power according to the will of the people.

This commemorative invitation celebrates the Inauguration of William Jefferson Clinton as President of the United States of America and Albert Gore, Jr. as Vice President of the United States of America. In presenting you with this commemorative invitation, we welcome your participation in any of the public events of The Fifty-Second Presidential Inaugural.

RONALD H. BROWN
CHAIRMAN

HARRY THOMASON
LINDA BLOODWORTH THOMASON
GENERAL CO-CHAIRS

RAHM EMANUEL
MARY MEL FRENCH
CO-EXECUTIVE DIRECTORS

FOR THE FIRST TIME IN HISTORY THE ENTIRE PRESIDENTIAL INAUGURAL INVITATION PACKAGE IS ENGRAVED AND PRINTED ON RECYCLED PAPER

THE 52ND PRESIDENTIAL INAUGURAL

AN AMERICAN REUNION

CALENDAR OF PUBLIC EVENTS

AMERICA'S REUNION ON THE MALL
SUNDAY, JANUARY 17, 1993
10:00 AM

•

CALL FOR REUNION
LINCOLN MEMORIAL
INAUGURAL CELEBRATION CONCERT AND FIREWORKS
SUNDAY, JANUARY 17, 1993
3:00 PM

•

THE AMERICAN GALA
THE CAPITAL CENTRE
MONDAY, JANUARY 18, 1993
7:30 PM

•

SALUTE TO CHILDREN
THE JOHN F. KENNEDY CENTER FOR THE PERFORMING ARTS
TUESDAY, JANUARY 19, 1993
1:30 PM UNTIL 2:30 PM

•

SALUTE TO YOUTH
THE JOHN F. KENNEDY CENTER FOR THE PERFORMING ARTS
TUESDAY, JANUARY 19, 1993
3:00 PM UNTIL 4:00 PM

•

INAUGURAL CEREMONY
UNITED STATES CAPITOL
WEDNESDAY, JANUARY 20, 1993
11:30 AM
OPEN TO THE PUBLIC FOR STANDING ROOM

•

PRESIDENTIAL INAUGURAL PARADE
UNITED STATES CAPITOL TO THE WHITE HOUSE
WEDNESDAY, JANUARY 20, 1993
2:00 PM

•

A PRESIDENTIAL OPEN HOUSE
THE WHITE HOUSE
THURSDAY, JANUARY 21, 1993
9:00 AM UNTIL 12:00 NOON

ALL EVENTS ARE FREE — AMERICAN GALA, SALUTE TO CHILDREN AND
SALUTE TO YOUTH REQUIRE TICKETS. PLEASE CALL 1-800-INAUG93

The Presidential Inaugural Committee
requests the honor of your presence
to attend and participate
in the
Inauguration of
William Jefferson Clinton
as
President of the United States of America
and
Albert Gore, Jr.
as
Vice President of the United States of America
on Wednesday, the twentieth of January
one thousand nine hundred and ninety-three
in the City of Washington

CHAPTER 16

RETIREMENT

Jerry retired in Encampment, WY

Jerry Michie to Retire

B. G. "Jerry" Michie has announced his plans to retire as Executive Director for the Wyoming County Commissioners Association (WCCA). Jerry has been an active member of county government for over 31 years. He served as Deputy County Assessor in Carbon County for six years prior to being elected to the position of Carbon County Treasurer in 1969. After serving as the County Treasurer for eight years, Jerry served two terms representing Carbon County in the Wyoming House of Representatives from 1979 to 1981.

Jerry Michie, Gene Wilson and Gene Calvert

In 1981, Jerry became the Executive Director for WCCA. His legislative experience has proven to be invaluable for WCCA. Jerry has provided exceptional leadership in introducing and supporting legislation involving Wyoming counties. Through the years, he has witnessed many changes involving county government and has been instrumental in many of these changes.

Jerry's leadership goes beyond his duties in Wyoming and his strong and supportive representation of Wyoming has been nationally recognized. In 1993, Jerry was elected President of the National Council of County Association Executives (NCCAE).

Jerry is a native of Rawlins and is a Navy Veteran of the Korean Conflict. He received his college education at Montana State University, Denver University and the University of Wyoming. Jerry has been an active supporter of the University of Wyoming through the Cowboy Joe Club and can be regularly found in the stands at UW football games. He has been active in Elks, V.F.W., D.A.V., American Legion, and Knights of Columbus.

Through his many years of public service, Jerry has helped maintain the quality of life we enjoy in Wyoming. When asked about his greatest accomplishments, he just smiles and says, "His three kids; Renee, Jerry Jr. and Geneva." Jerry plans to return to Carbon County and make Encampment his new home upon retirement.

Best of luck Jerry! Thanks for your active support of T^2.

PROCLAMATION

WHEREAS, Wyoming is fortunate to have had a dedicated public servant working on our behalf for over thirty years; and

WHEREAS, that public servant, B.G. "Jerry" Michie, a native of Rawlins, Wyoming, began his career serving in the U.S. Navy during the Korean Conflict; and

WHEREAS, Jerry has served Carbon County, Wyoming and the nation as Deputy Carbon County Assessor, Carbon County Treasurer, Wyoming State Legislator, Executive Director for the Wyoming County Commissioners Association and was last year elected President of the National Council of County Association Executives; and

WHEREAS, Jerry is a proud native of Wyoming serving as a member of the Elks, V.F.W., D.A.V., American Legion, Knights of Columbus and the Cowboy Joe Club and in addition a good family man raising three fine children on his own; and

WHEREAS, Wyoming is indebted to Jerry Michie and is thankful for his many years of service to his native state. We bid him a fond farewell as he enters his much deserved retirement.

NOW THEREFORE, I, MIKE SULLIVAN, Governor of the State of Wyoming, do hereby proclaim November 12, 1994, to be

"JERRY MICHIE DAY"

in Wyoming in honor of this fine gentleman and his deserved retirement.

IN WITNESS WHEREOF, I have hereunto set my hand and caused the Great Seal of the State of Wyoming to be affixed this 10th day of October, 1994.

_____
Governor

_____
Secretary of State

November 1, 1994

Mr. Jerry Michie
Wyoming County Commissioners Association
PO Box 86
Cheyenne, WY 82003

Dear Jerry:

I understand Wyoming is giving you a "little" party on the occasion of your retirement. Well, I wish I could be there to celebrate with all the great people of Wyoming. I know from the opportunities you gave me to visit with the WCCA in Sheridan that it is going to be a great time on the old town tonight! And they are giving your recognition you richly deserve -- as a Wyoming leader and a national leader.

We are going to miss you in the National Association of Counties. We're going to miss your political instincts, your political toughness, and above all your wonderful Irish wit and the twinkle in your one good Irish eye!

You have earned the greatest of respect from me and members of the NACo Board during your services these past two years. You have been an uncompromising supporter of the role of county government as the centerpiece of our political and governmental system. We have benefitted greatly by your quiet work in building consensus among the Board on divisive issues. With a Board of 100 members that's no small task!

On behalf of all the counties, particularly those in the west with large federal land ownership, I want to publicly recognize you in front of all your friends for the successful efforts you made to bring the eastern state associations into the battle for fairness in federal payments in lieu of taxes. I agree with you that without their help, we could not have succeeded -- and you were the key to that networking with state associations across the country during your term as President of the National Conference of County Association Executives. Over $100 million per year in long overdue payments to counties will finally be made for the loss of local taxes which come with federal ownership of land.

I would also ask you to express my gratitude to the Wyoming congressional delegation -- Senator Wallop, Senator Simpson and Representative Thomas for their critical support and assistance in the successful passage of this legislation. I know you will not believe me but it just goes to show you Jerry, that we Republicans aren't all bad!

Judge Dale White joins me in wishing you the best. We have valued your friendship. It won't be the same not to hear that invitation to "stick with me and you'll go places...it may be out of town on a rail but you'll be movin'!". Well, as you take your ride on the rails please don't forget to stop by and visit all your friends in county government.

Best wishes to you, my friend. May all the good things come your way as you take on a new phase in your life.

Sincerely,

Randall Franke, President
National Association of Counties

1 Street, NW

81

HOUSE OF REPRESENTATIVES
WASHINGTON, D.C. 20515

CRAIG THOMAS
WYOMING

November 12, 1994

Congratulations Jerry!

This is a special night for you and you've earned it.
After all your years in public service, it's hard to
imagine what it's going to be like not having you in
the usual place. It will take some getting used to
and you'll be missed.

Jerry, your presence and influence have touched many.
You have a unique and singular role in the State of
Wyoming. Your service to Carbon County and at the
Legislature, your good work for the County Commissioners,
the distinction of your presidency of the National
Association of Executive Directors -- all speak of
your dedication to our Wyoming brand of local govern-
ment.

I'm sorry we can't be here tonight to share in this
tribute to you. Your friends and family are very proud
of you -- that's certainly evident -- and they have good
reason to be. Jerry, best wishes to you for this next
adventure of yours. May your coming years be full of
friendship, laughter and love -- and full of the things
you now have time to enjoy!

Best of personal regards.

Craig Thomas
Member of Congress

Jerry and Craig Thomas

MALCOLM WALLOP
WYOMING

COMMITTEES:

RGY AND NATURAL RESOURCES
FINANCE
SMALL BUSINESS
INTELLIGENCE

United States Senate
WASHINGTON, DC 20510-5001

WASHINGTON OFFICE (202) 2
CASPER OFFICE (307) 2
 2201 FEDERAL BUILDING B
CHEYENNE OFFICE (307) 6
 2009 FEDERAL CENTER 82
LANDER OFFICE (307) 3
 POST OFFICE BUILDING 82
ROCK SPRINGS OFFICE (307) 3
 2515 FOOTHILL BLVD. 821
SHERIDAN OFFICE (307) 6
 40 SOUTH MAIN 82801

November 10, 1994

Jerry Michie
409 West 24th Street
Cheyenne, Wyoming 82001

Dear Jerry:

As you celebrate this evening, I would like to recognize you for your fourteen years of dedicated service to the Wyoming County Commissioners Association. Commendation is also warranted for participating in the democratic process throughout your entire career as the President of the National Association of Executive Directors, the Deputy Carbon County Assessor, the Carbon County Treasurer and as a Wyoming State Legislator.

After all these many years of noteworthy public service, your retirement is certainly well deserved.

Congratulations and best wishes to you and your family for happiness and fulfillment in the years to come.

Sincerely,

Malcolm Wallop
Malcolm Wallop
United States Senator

MW/po

Jerry and Malcom Wallop

Al Simpson
United States Senator
WASHINGTON, D.C. 20510

November 10, 1994

Mr. Bernard G. Michie
409 West 24th Street
Cheyenne, Wyoming 82001

Dear Jerry:

My spies are out! Someone came up to me
the other day and said, "Did you know Jerry is
retiring?" I was a bit surprised by the comment
and replied, "Yes, I do know Jerry -- and he is
anything <u>but</u> retiring!"

Now that the news has fully "sunk in", I
understand that a nice little celebration will
be held to commemorate your many years of public
service. It sounds like a grand event. Ann and
I so wish that it were possible to join you and
all of your friends and family who are gathered
to roast and toast you. Unfortunately, various
long-scheduled activities will prevent that.

Over the years I have been at quite a few
of these kinds of events. I hope you are
properly prepared, Jerry! So often your best
friends will come up to the podium and tell the
most outlandish tales about you. But be
forewarned -- there is a method they follow!
First they toast you a little -- to get you good
and blasted -- and just when you're feeling
good, the <u>roasting</u> starts. You get placed on
the spit and roasted to a golden brown -- and
through it all you must sit and smile while all
sorts of barbs are popped right in your mush!

Jerry Michie
Page Two

But there is a bright side! After the roasting is done, you then have the opportunity to get up and tell 'em your side! So I hope you are busy loading your cannon with all sorts of juicy tidbits. When your host introduces you, the "rest of the story" will be heard!

If I were in attendance tonight, I would have to put aside my "roasts" in favor of my "toasts." You are one of the "good guys" and I have greatly enjoyed having the opportunity to come to know you and work with you.

I would offer up the first toast to honor you for the spirited way you participate in your government. You are a special guy and you learned at an early age that "Democracy is not a spectator sport." That has been a motto that you have adhered to and "kept" all these years while you've been a player in the game of politics.

I would then toast you for the fine example you are to so many others. You have never hesitated to "wade in and get wet all over" whenever there was a problem that needed fixing. You were always one to get involved to the fullest extent possible.

About then, I think my time would be running out. So I will finish by offering one more toast to you, Jerry. Retirement will be a good thing. It will find you reflecting on the rich and pleasant memories of the past -- and making new memories as you continue your active and fulfilling life. Just know that the thoughts and best wishes of so many in the community go out to you at this significant time in your life.

Jerry Michie
Page Three

   Congratulations, Jerry. You have a
lifetime of outstanding service and commitment
to your family, your community, your state and
your country to look back on. We are very proud
of you! Ann joins in sending our kindest wishes
and hopes that you will thoroughly enjoy your
retirement.

                              Your friend

                              Alan K. Simpson
                              United States Senator

AKS/jag

Jerry and Alan Simpson

Key to all the Cities of Wyoming

Bernard Gerard "Jerry" or "BG" Michie

January 26, 1932–February 19,2008

Bernard G. Michie
1932-2008

Bernard Gerard "Jerry" Michie died Feb. 19 at the age of 76 at the Veterans Affairs Medical Center in Cheyenne.

Jerry was born Jan. 26, 1932, in Rawlins, the son of David F. Michie Sr. and Grace Vivette (Madden) Michie.

He attended and graduated from Rawlins High School in 1950. He attended Montana State University on a football scholarship.

Upon the outbreak of the Korean War, he enlisted in the Navy, where he served two terms, suffering the loss of an eye. After a stay in the Naval Hospital in San Diego, he returned to Wyoming and attended the University of Wyoming and Denver University.

After college, he had many occupations, until a mentor of his advised him to "use his brains rather than his fists." He then began his many years of public service, beginning as the deputy county assessor, county treasurer and two terms as state representative, all for Carbon County. In 1982, he became the executive director of the Wyoming County Commissioners Association.

He served as national president of the National Association of County Executives. He also served on many public boards and committees before his retirement in 1994.

Jerry was also involved in his community and was especially involved with youth sports, including youth baseball, high-school sports and the University of Wyoming. He was a single parent of three children. He will remain in everyone's heart as a great human being and will be missed by all.

Jerry is survived by a daughter, Renee Bohl (Mike), a son, Jerry Michie Jr., and a daughter, Geneva Michie, all of Cheyenne. He is also survived by one brother, Dr. David F. Michie (Betsy) of Rawlins; stepchildren, Cora Maxwell and Chet Stagner; five grandchildren; two great-grandchildren; many nephews, nieces and great friends.

He was preceded in death by his parents, David F. Michie Sr. and Grace Vivette Michie; five brothers, James, David F. Jr., John, Tom and Fran; and four sisters, Ellen, Rachel, Alice and Marge.

A rosary service will be 5:30 p.m. Friday at St. Joseph's Catholic Church in Rawlins with Mass of Christian Burial at 10 a.m. Saturday at St. Joseph Catholic Church in Rawlins with Father Sam Hayes as the celebrant.

Burial will follow at Rawlins Cemetery.

Pallbearers will be Jeremy Larson, Dillon Karajanis, David Michie, Chris Michie, Bill Michie, Chris Karajanis and Truland Eyre.

Honorary pallbearers will be Gary Eyre, Melvin Forney, Darrell Stubbs, Ron Holloway, Vern Holloway, Lyle McCallister and Bill Vasey.

This is a paid obituary.

DAVE FREUDENTHAL
GOVERNOR

THE STATE OF WYOMING

STATE CAPITOL
CHEYENNE, WY 82002

Office of the Governor

February 26, 2008

Mrs. Renee Bohl
c/o Mike Bohl
Wyoming Bank & Trust
5827 Yellowstone Road
Cheyenne, WY 82009

Dear Renee,

  I am writing to convey Nancy's and my sympathy on the passing of Jerry. We have wonderful memories of Jerry – the old days with Ed Herschler, and the Carbon County mafia, Jerry's time with the commissioners and the Democratic Party.

  Most importantly, Jerry was a great friend – a caring, compassionate human being. His love of life and people were unmistakable and contagious. We will miss him but we cherish his memory.

        Best regards,

        Dave Freudenthal
        Governor

DF:pjb

TTY: 777-7860   PHONE: (307) 777-7434   FAX: (307) 632-3909

ALAN K. SIMPSON

United States Senator (Ret.)
WYOMING

March 26, 2008

Renee & Michael Bohl
906 Frontier Park Avenue
Cheyenne, WY 82001

Geneva Michie
815 Foyer Avenue
Cheyenne, WY 82001

Bernard Michie, Jr.
909 W. College Drive
Cheyenne, WY 82007

To the Family of Jerry Michie:

I was so saddened to learn recently of the death of my old friend Jerry.

I first met him when we were both in athletics – he in Rawlins High and me in Cody High, but all we knew about Jerry and the Rawlins Outlaws was that he was one hell of an athlete! And he surely was. But he was also a helluva fine person.

If you could sum up his persona, it would be in words like: Loyal, patriotic, involved, caring, bright, warm, wise, witty – and a friend to his friends.

He just always seemed to be involved with so many things and always did it with that big smile and that big heart.

We didn't see a great deal of each other in these latter years but each and every time we did it was always a warm and wonderful greeting with an old friend. My life is richer for having shared a small portion of it with him.

I just wanted you to know these things. Our thoughts and prayers go winging out to you and my wife Ann joins in sending our love and sympathy to all of you and to all of your dear ones.

Not Printed at Government expense

Affable and effective
Politician was advocate for county government

By JOAN BARRON
Star-Tribune capital bureau

One Wyoming life
A weekly profile of a recently deceased Wyoming resident.

MICHIE

CHEYENNE — Bernard G. "Jerry" Michie was a witty, affable and smart politician and a crack lobbyist.

He also was a loving father to three children he raised as a single parent when their mother left, said Michie's daughter, Renee Bohl.

She said her father was one of the first men to get custody of their children in the 1960s. He was a devout Catholic and never remarried.

Michie was deputy county assessor, county treasurer and served two terms as a Democratic state representative, all from Carbon County.

In 1982 he became executive director of the Wyoming County Commissioners Association and served as national president of the National Association of County Executives.

After he retired in 1994, he moved to Encampment and later to Arizona, where his daughter, Renee, lives part time.

When his health failed, he said he wanted to return to Wyoming even though the altitude wasn't good for him, she said.

Michie died at the Veterans Affairs Medical Center in Cheyenne on Feb. 19 at age 76.

His funeral wasn't held until last month because his daughter, Renee, was in Australia at the time of his death.

Michie's mentor was R.L. "Reno" Hakala, who was Carbon County assessor and later was appointed by Gov. Ed Herschler to be one of the three members of the old Wyoming Tax Commission, Michie's daughter said.

Michie graduated from Rawlins High School in 1950 and attended Montana State University on a football scholarship.

After the outbreak of the Korean War, Michie enlisted in the Navy, where he served two hitches.

He suffered the loss of one eye while serving on a destroyer. The ship was returning from a tour but hadn't yet reached San Diego when a guy hit him on the back, Michie's daughter said.

The ship had bunk beds attached by chains with hooks on the end. Michie fell into the hook and spent nearly a year in the naval hospital at San Diego.

He always said he lost the eye in the "Battle of San Diego."

"With that eye, you never told him to keep an eye on anything," his daughter said. "He would take it out and put it in your drink or in your seat."

Joe Evans, who succeeded Michie as director of the Wyoming County Commissioners Association, said his predecessor liked working at the national level and was very involved in the passage of changes in the federal Payment in Lieu of Taxes program.

State Sen. Bill Vasey of Rawlins said Michie was an effective lobbyist for the county commissioners.

"He was really an intelligent guy. He could look at a bill and understand what it did," he said.

When he got out of the Navy, Michie was a "tough guy," Vasey said. At that time Rawlins was a tough place to be.

"Reno Hakala gathered him up and said, 'You know you can either hang around Front Street and get in trouble or you can use your mind,'" Vasey said.

That's when Michie went to work for county government.

Former Secretary of State Kathy Karpan, who grew up in Rawlins, said Michie was an effective, well-respected lobbyist because of his experience at the county level.

"He had the affability that we associate with a successful Irish political figure," Karpan said. "Every time you saw Jerry, he had a smile and very self-deprecating humor."

Michie is also survived by a son, Jerry Michie Jr., and a daughter, Geneva Michie, both of Cheyenne, and a brother, Dr. David F. Michie of Rawlins.

He was buried at the Rawlins cemetery.

Contact Joan Barron at joan.barron@trib.com or by phone at 307-632-1244.

Jerry was such an awesome man... a rock hard pillar in our community!

He used to be the public speaker at all the Outlaw football, basketball games and then he even did the Babe Ruth baseball games at the Sunny side park! He always did a fine job, he was an expert.

He was one of the instrumental men in bringing Rawlins Little League Football; and he always had one hell of a team as the head coach!

He and Ronny Holloway took me to my first NCAA I football game in Laramie. How exciting!

The Michie clan are somehow related to the Kulmus Group!!!

Love BG forever!!!

By Mark Kulmus

Bill Vasey
I don't think know how tough a town rawlins was after the war and Rawlins only had 5 or 6 police men and they didn't come down to front or 4th street so the bar owners were charged with keeping the piece and your dad was othe main enforcers he was the good guy as kids we would hang around the bars waiting to see the action as he throw out a drunk. The other thing was how good he was as the county assesor fair and through.

Epilogue

Just a few memories of my Uncle Jerry from his loving nephew, Bill Michie.

Jerry was always "on" with something funny to say. He told me many stories and he did many hilarious things in my presence. One story he liked to tell involved him at a national meeting of the County Commissioners Associations from across the land. Representing the state of Wyoming which starts with the letter "W," Jerry was sitting at the opening of this national meeting, listening to each state in alphabetical order come to the, microphone and tell of the wondrous things they had done in the previous year to make their work more timely and relevant. Jerry said most of them were telling about what terrific computer systems they had installed and how that had made life so much better for their organization.

Since Jerry did not even own a computer at that time, he puzzled about what to say when they finally got to him. Then he had a momentous inspiration. Eventually, they reached the letter "W" and Wyoming's representative was called forward. He said that he started by praising all the wonderful things that other states were doing and how impressive those things were...But then he said that Wyoming had done something far more impressive and practical than anyone else in the room. He described how in Wyoming they looked at their members and subsequently changed the seating arrangement to put two special members of the association seated next to each other. One member from the northern part of the state had lost his right arm in a tragic accident. The other member had lost his left arm in an agricultural accident. So, these members were seated next to each other. The member without a right arm was seated to the left of the member without a left arm. As he explained this, he held his arms out and brought them together in a clap while explaining that from that moment on they were able to join in when everyone else clapped.

What followed this was silence as the members in the auditorium sat stunned at what Jerry had just said and done. Then the room exploded with cheers and laughter as they caught the humor. They gave him a standing ovation. Later they elected him President Pro Tem of the National Association and everyone wanted to meet him personally!

In a subsequent year at another national meeting in Austin, Texas he was an invited guest to the man who started the Big "O" tire company. Big O had just built himself a splendid mansion and during the meal, he turned to Jerry and asked, "How do you like my new digs?" Jerry was more interested in the pork chop on the plate in front of him so as he explained to me, he did not even look up but casually answered Oscar that he thought it was going to be a nice house when he finished it. The Big O at first just stared at Jerry who was doing real justice to that pork chop...then Oscar realized what had just happened and laughed uproariously. Jerry wasn't much for small talk when good food was present.

Once I was sitting with Jerry and big Bill Vasey in the Square Shooters Café. Those two always carefully planned where to sit. It had to be in the center of one's view when entering the restaurant but not too close and not too far in the back. There was one table that met those requirements perfectly and that is where we were sitting when a man with a small group of people entered the front door. Upon seeing him, Jerry and Bill went into politician mode immediately, but they couldn't remember the man's name. They instantly started recounting what they did remember. Stuff like, "I worked with him on that water project...and, yes, he was on such and such committee." Meanwhile, the man spotted us and was headed towards our table. Then it hit them...they remembered his name! They both jumped up onto their feet and greeted the man by his first name like it had been just yesterday since they had seen him. What an old friend! (I thought to myself...these two are masterful politicians...and they were!)

On another occasion, while sitting at the same table in the same restaurant, Tony Rose walked in and headed right for Jerry and me. Tony was the police chief and a state congressman, but he had recently accepted a position with the Federal Marshalls in Cheyenne and had to give up his seat in congress. He greeted both of us and then, after initial niceties, turned to Jerry and said, "You need to tell Bill here to toss his hat into the ring to be my replacement in the legislature.

Without a pause, Jerry exclaimed, "No!" Tony looked stunned as that was not the reaction he expected. Gathering his composure, Tony asked, "Why not?" Again, without a pause, Jerry answered, "Because then we would have to publicly admit that we have a Republican in our family." Jerry kept a straight face...After a moment or two, Tony realized that he had been played and we all shared a good laugh.

I will sum this up with a short story Jerry told that had happened to him on his return to Rawlins after his first term in the state legislature. He said that one of the local "movers and shakers" approached him and asked, "Well, Jerry, what did you learn in your first experience with the legislature?" Jerry said that he thought for a moment and then responded, "The most relevant thing I learned was that not all Republicans are devils and that not all Democrats are angels..."

That really sums up my Uncle Jerry. He could work with people of all persuasions. He was open to hear people he agreed with and was equally open to those with whom he shared little agreement. We could use more like him in our present day and age!!!

POEMS

BY

B.G. "Jerry " Michie

WYOMING

O Wyoming! O Wyoming! 0 Wyoming!

Tried and True

O Wyoming! O Wyoming! OWyoming!

Skies of Blue

Frost your mountains
Rain your prairies
Let the winds come blowing through

Fish your rivers
Hunt your valleys
Leave the land as good as new

Ring out all your awesome glory
Praise the western rendezvous
the western rendezvous
And Watch the sunsets fade from view

Lock these moments in your
Memory Feel the power surge
Know that God is touching you.

O Wyoming! O Wyoming! O Wyoming!

I Love You

AMERICA

Good Morning!
Isn't it Great to be an
American!! I'm Proud to be
an American This
Great Country of
Freedoms,
Set down by the Declaration of Independence guaranteed by Our Constitution and Bill of
Rights
We don't have Kings or Queens
or Dictators Our symbol is our
Flag

Printed in the United States
by Baker & Taylor Publisher Services